Always Allie   1/23/15

Cindi,

A dog is not our whole life, but they can make our life whole!

Hope to have you on board!

Dr. Kipp

Always Allie

Dr. Kipp A. Van Camp

Published by:

Cognitive Publishing, LLC
1230 SW Harvey St., Suite B
Topeka, KS 66604-4070

Printed by: Walsworth Publishing, 803 S. Missouri Ave., Marceline, MO 64658

 Always Allie. Copyright © 2011 by Dr. Kipp A. Van Camp

Cover Design by Tim Lynch

Book Composition by Steve Brooker @ Just Your Type

For information about special discounts or bulk purchases, please contact Special Sales at www.alwaysallie.com.

Library of Congress Cataloging-in-Publication Data

New ISBN 13: 978-0-615-49636-8
New ISBN 10: 0-61-549636-9
Previous edition cataloged as follows:

Van Camp, Kipp A., 1962-

       Always Allie/Kipp A. Van Camp –

1st ed.

p. cm.

ISBN-13: 978-0-615-49636-8

ISBN-10: 0-61-549636-9

    1.   Bichon Frise-Kansas-Biography. 2. Van Camp, Kipp A., 1962-

  I.   Title.

1-443793861
ISBN 13: 978-0-615-49636-8   ISBN 10: 0-61-549636-9

                                      2010913374

Printed in the United States of America

This book is dedicated to

To the Helping Hands Humane Society of Topeka, Kansas,
and to all the homeless dogs who have been forsaken.

To my wife, Tracy, my two sons, Kolby and Weston,
each member of our family, and all our family pets.

To our four-legged daughter, Chelsea Alexis; you filled us with
a lifetime of love and memories. In our eyes, you were *Always Allie*.

Contents

Introduction

Have you ever had a uniquely pure and genuine relationship that completely absorbed you both emotionally and spiritually? For the better part of the past two decades, I had the good fortune of experiencing such a profound and lasting relationship with our Bichon Frise, Chelsea Alexis (Allie).

My dad was a veterinarian, and I'd been around animals all my growing-up life. But during those hectic years spent in medical school, residency and practice, Allie quickly became more than a pet. As strange as it may sound, she became my teacher, my life-coach and my therapist.

In spite of being a student of human behavior, I had failed to truly appreciate how our pets affect each of us. At least until Allie came along and began my personal instruction.

Authorities on animal behavior have studied in great detail the human-animal bond. I had even casually observed a special interaction between some of Dad's clients and their owners. But it wasn't until Allie wrapped me tightly around her furry little paw that I began to fully comprehend the depth and authentic innocence of the human-animal relationship.

There are many claims from the scientific community that the right pet can even lower an owner's blood pressure, or assist in battling depression. After a stressful day at the office listening to my patients' physical ailments and general woes, Allie had a similar effect on my own vital signs. She curled up next to me. Several minutes of stroking her fur, and I could feel my muscles relaxing and the tension leaving my strained body.

The first time I saw Allie, I knew she was that extraordinary dog who would steal our hearts and fill us with a lifetime of love and cherished memories.

Allie was an integral part of me, my family and my work for seventeen years. During that time, she taught me how to live more fully and how to love more completely. When she died, I was devastated. But I was also inspired to keep her with me, to share her wisdom and to keep her alive.

Only hours after Allie died, on March 13, 2009, I sat down and began to write Allie's story. Telling her story came naturally. The book became a tribute to Allie and a love letter to my wife, Tracy. In putting Allie's story on paper, I could, perhaps, memorialize my four-legged, furry daughter, who, against all odds, stole my heart. Who could have guessed how much a twelve-pound canine would challenge me in all aspects of my life. She showed me how to relax, she encouraged me to enjoy life more fully, and she taught me how to love more deeply.

By reading about Allie, I hope you will reflect on your own teachers and guides and revel in all the wisdom they've shared with you. Her zest for life, her infectious character, and her independent spirit, made her Always Allie, the feisty little dog who changed our world.
I hope you will also benefit from some of the lessons I learned from a seemingly innocent little ball of fur, the powerhouse that changed my life, Allie.

While four-legged friends definitely enrich our lives, occasionally, owners find themselves wishing Fido came with an instruction manual. To this end, I've included a handy resource section, *Tidbits and Treats*, at the back of the book. From how to select the most compatible breed, to determining the qualities of a qualified obedience trainer, veterinary caregiver, and more, these topics are relevant to first-time as well as seasoned pet owners. If only I'd had such a resource when Allie first joined our family! The suggestions are discussed in detail on our website, www.alwaysallie.com.

"No matter how little money and how few possessions you own, having a dog makes you rich."

Louis Sabin

CHAPTER 1

Allie Arrives: *The Perfect Present*

"Mom, I'd like you to do something very important for me. I want you to find just the right dog for Tracy. I want it to be a surprise for Christmas."

"That doesn't sound too difficult," Mom replied.

"It might be harder than you think," I warned. "Tracy grew up with German Shepherds and wants a big dog. A big dog is not practical in our apartment. Can you find a small, sturdy dog that doesn't shed and would make a good companion?"

It was September 1991. Tracy and I were newlyweds living in a two-bedroom apartment in St. Louis, Missouri. Having finished medical school, I had just started my internship in general medicine and was spending more nights at the hospital than at home. I wanted to get Tracy a canine companion to keep her company.

Mom had always been the one to pick out our family pets. She grew up on a farm and had spent much of her time around animals. She also assisted Dad with his veterinary practice. Back in my hometown of

Colby, Kansas, her reputation had grown to "pet whisperer" status. She had a knack for placing the right pet with the right owner.

Mom accepted the challenge.

In late October she called. "I found just the right breed! A Bichon Frise (Bee-shahn Free-zay.)" She enunciated the two words very clearly.

"I've never heard of that breed. What's it like?"

"Similar to a poodle, but sturdier with a stockier build. They have adorable personalities and look like they are smiling and laughing all of the time."

This sounded interesting. "What color are they?"

"White."

"Sounds like we're talking about the right breed!"

"Why don't you look up and study 'Bichon Frise'?" Mom suggested, in her usual motherly tone.

I did just that. I went to the library and studied about the Bichon Frise. And sure enough, the breed was just what I had been looking for.

Over the next several weeks, I dropped hints to Tracy about her Christmas present. "I've found just the right gift for you. I know it's early, but I came across it on sale, and I couldn't resist getting it. The only problem is it was on sale, and if you don't like it, you can't return it."

Tracy was curious, but I refused to tell her more. This went on until Christmas.

I couldn't stop thinking about this present. On several occasions I nearly spilled the beans. In order to appease my burning desire to tell Tracy about this puppy, I contacted Mom every chance I got. I figured the more I knew about the puppy and the selection process, the easier it would be for me to relax. It started innocently with an occasional phone call once or twice a week. But as the excitement and intrigue grew, I started to call her every other day. This ultimately progressed to two calls a day, morning and night.

After nearly one week of these incessant interruptions, Mom finally said: "Don't you have anything else to do with your time? I thought interns were busy saving lives or learning about disease!"

I got the hint. I forced myself to be patient.

In late November Mom called. "I've located a litter of four Bichon puppies in Denver, Colorado. They'll be ready to wean the first week of December. The price is reasonable, and the sire and dame are American Kennel Club registered."

"That sounds great. Let's get one! Don't you think a female would be better than the male?"

"Absolutely! I'll call tomorrow and make arrangements to pick one out."

Over the following days, I felt like an expectant father awaiting the arrival of his adopted child. I was about to burst. All the while, I couldn't let Tracy in on my secret.

On December 5, Mom called. "I just got home from Denver. I found just the right puppy. She's adorable—the pick of the litter." I could hear her excitement. "Your sister and I will go back to Denver next week and get her. We'll start potty training after we pick her up. The puppy, that is," Mom chuckled at her own joke.

I could hardly wait to surprise Tracy with the new puppy. I found myself distracted at work. Keeping a secret of this significance was eating me up inside. I received a daily update from my mom, my sister Kim, and even my father.

The excitement of getting a puppy thrilled me. I envisioned us playing fetch and taking long strolls together. We would be the best of friends.

This was our first Christmas as a married couple. We celebrated Christmas Eve with Tracy's family in St. Louis. Then we got up before dawn and headed the ten hours due west to Colby, arriving around three o'clock on Christmas afternoon.

My pent-up excitement now changed to full-blown anxiety. What if Tracy didn't like the puppy? We hadn't even talked about getting a pet. What if she didn't want the responsibility of a dog? What if she felt a Bichon was too wimpy? It's not a German Shepherd! I spent the last hour of the trip trying to silence the demons in my head.

Once home, I greeted everyone, then told Tracy I wanted to check on her gift. Kim hurried me upstairs and introduced me. The ball of pristine white fur, black nose and beautifully expressive dark eyes were perfect. I fell in love immediately.

The little puppy licked me, and we played for a moment. She had a meek bark and a playful growl, more cute than ferocious. Instantly, I was a proud father.

Kim had orchestrated things to a tee. She found a container about the size of a large hatbox with a removable lid. She wrapped the box and lid in traditional red Christmas wrapping and put a bow on top. With the puppy inside, this made the perfect Christmas package.

I raced into my parents' family room with the present in my hands. Tracy sat on the couch.

"What's the big hurry?" she asked.

I handed the box to Tracy. And as she took hold, the puppy moved. Cautiously, she lifted the lid. The puppy popped out of the box, licked Tracy on the nose, and a love affair of seventeen and a half years began.

We named her Chelsea Alexis after her mother, whose name was Chelsea's Cupcake. Allie was everything I had hoped. She had just the right personality for Tracy and me. Plus, she instinctively understood that she was Tracy's gift, a role she took seriously.

Around eleven that night, we got ready for bed. Tracy picked up Allie, hugged her and placed her in her kennel at the foot of the bed.

"She's so cute," Tracy said. "But I feel strongly about keeping her in her kennel at night. I'd rather she not sleep in our bed."

The words had barely left Tracy's mouth when Allie started to whimper. We lay there silently, listening to Allie whine.

What happened next was more telling of our future with Allie than I could have imagined. Tracy got out of bed, lifted Allie out of the kennel and placed her on a pillow between the two of us. The whimpering instantly ceased.

Allie stared at Tracy for a moment, then turned toward me. The expression on her face spoke loudly: Because of her good nature, she would allow us to sleep in her bed. She would sleep between us each and every night for the rest of her days. In record time, Allie established the official family hierarchy. She was in charge, Tracy was nearly the boss, and I had lost all significance.

CHAPTER 2

Training in Child Rearing: *Doc vs. Dog*

We had read about the importance of routines and took our roles as new doggie parents seriously. We fed Allie twice a day. She had a ravenous appetite.

Within a few days, her clock was set. At six A.M., Allie's internal alarm went off in unison with my physical alarm clock. She graciously gave me time to shower and shave before demanding my undivided attention regarding her personal needs.

We assumed the daunting task of potty training that Kim had begun. It didn't take long to recognize Allie's independence. She was a smart little dog. She had a natural instinct to do what was right. She immediately understood that "wetting and pooping" on the floor was not acceptable. Getting her to potty outside was easy. Establishing exactly where Allie would relieve herself was the challenge.

I had never heard Tracy described as a morning person. She was a teacher and needed every minute to get ready for school, so I assumed the role of walking Allie each morning. I took Allie into the back courtyard directly outside our ground-floor apartment. With her first step into the great outdoors, Allie burst into action. She sniffed and searched the entire grounds until she had found the perfect spot to "go."

The first few mornings I exercised extreme tolerance and understanding. This didn't last. Clearly, her behavior was more than the playful curiosity of an adorable puppy; it was the sheer determination and independence of a willful dog.

This morning routine continued for months, regardless of the weather or the inconvenience to my busy schedule. We repeated the same process every night before bed. Two times a day, Allie and I headed to the grassy courtyard behind our apartment. With each trip, I coaxed and encouraged her to do her business—all of it. All the while she dug in, determined to make a game of how long we could wander around. Allie pulled on her leash, her actions defiant!

I had read that dogs often take on the personality of their owner. Was this some type of test? Was Allie already displaying some of my own traits? Was she mimicking my willfulness? Was she mocking me with her obstinence? No, she must be imitating Tracy, I jokingly told myself.

What about that age-old adage that dogs wanted to please their master?

Whenever I questioned this, Tracy reminded me that Allie didn't drag *her* all over the yard at dawn or in the dark of night. Allie got right down to business when she was with her.

I spent most of the daylight hours at the hospital engaged in medical training. Perhaps Allie could relate to my work ethic. I, on the other hand, could only dream of having her enthusiasm.

Like most puppies, Allie was energetic and easily excitable. She loved to play. She was growing rapidly and had already doubled in size. Full grown she would weigh about twelve pounds.

She loved to chew. One afternoon, left alone, she chewed the varnish off the legs of Tracy's wooden rocking chair. We were only gone for an hour. How could a tiny ball of fur cause such destruction in such a short time?

We searched for a deterrent. Being an intern in medicine, I devised a clever idea. I tied a soft chew bone to a two-inch Ace bandage and tied the loose end of the elastic wrap to a door handle, serving as an anchor for this inexpensive toy.

Allie quickly learned to stretch the Ace wrap and bone and then let go. The bone would ricochet, bouncing off anything in its path. She took great pleasure in this, racing around in circles each time she released the bone, never growing weary. I enjoyed this mindless entertainment, too.

At these moments of playful engagement, I realized Allie could teach me some valuable life lessons. I had always been driven. Some had accused me of being unable to relax and enjoy life. Allie somehow understood this and considered it her personal duty to teach me how to stop and smell the roses—even if her idea of roses was an Ace wrap and a cloth bone.

With a tube sock pulled over my hand, I could make the lifeless sock puppet instantly come alive, attacking Allie from behind. She thoroughly enjoyed this cat-and-mouse game, and whenever she caught the sock, she tore into it—and my hand—as if she had just captured the day's catch. (Bichons were originally bred for hunting. They chased small game like rabbits and squirrels. Or sock puppets.)

One evening after work, I sat on the floor of our apartment playing with Allie. As I jerked my stocking-covered hand from Allie's mouth, suddenly a tooth popped out. I was stunned. Why had this happened? How was it possible that a healthy puppy could have such poor teeth? Had I pulled too hard? Maybe she had a terrible illness, like leukemia, or some bone demineralization.

I called to Tracy, and soon we were both prying open Allie's mouth to look inside, something Allie thought was a game. After some time, and no obvious explanation for Allie's dental condition, my fears grew too great, so I called my dad.

"Does Allie have some kind of terrible illness?" I asked. "We were playing tug-of-war, and a tooth popped out."

"Well, I wouldn't get too worked up," my father advised. "I believe she'll lose many more. Her baby teeth will fall out and be replaced by her permanent ones."

I hung up the phone, but his words dwelled in my mind. I had finished medical school, was more than half-way through my internship, and somehow had failed to remember that all mammals have two sets of teeth, their baby teeth and their permanent. Mark Twain's advice, "better to keep your mouth closed and be assumed a fool than to open your mouth and remove all doubt," came to mind.

Sure enough, over the next several weeks, Allie lost all her baby teeth one by one. I had a great deal to learn as a doctor, and Tracy and I had a lot to learn as parents. Then it dawned on me: Allie would begin our training program in child rearing. She would teach us basic parenting skills before our children arrived.

CHAPTER 3

She Rules the School: *Obedience Lessons*

Dog lovers are an interesting breed. They talk to their pet in baby talk. They allow their dog to lick various anatomic structures upon its own body and turn around and lick their mouth, without any apparent concern for dog germs. Even though I never thought of myself in this light, Allie quickly showed me that neither Tracy nor I was any different. The first time I started speaking to Allie in baby talk, I felt rather foolish. But when Allie hopped up on Tracy's lap and licked her in the face, and Tracy responded to Allie's affection using her silly, childish voice, I realized I was in good company.

Allie was very demanding. Much of our time was spent giving her attention. Whenever I sat down to read, she would force herself between me and the newspaper or magazine. She did not accept "No" as a reasonable answer. She believed that we were placed on this earth to respond to her whims and desires. If I had a snack, she wanted one, too.

Also, while we were making progress in some areas of her training, like "stay," we were failing in many other ways. She continued to chew incessantly. She was now leaving little teeth marks on most of the furniture, some shoes, and even clothing. She was also leaving little scratch marks on the bottom of the doors whenever we left her in the bathroom or laundry room. Scratching the door was her method of protesting her confinement.

Allie's behavioral issues, though trying, had remained cute up to this point, but after the destruction of several pairs of shoes, we knew something had to give. We had to get a handle on these behaviors, but how? Tracy's friend had a suggestion: puppy school.

That's it, we thought. That's exactly what Allie needed—a little old-fashioned discipline.

I recalled my folks threatening my siblings and me with military school during our periods of disobedience. That was my perception of canine obedience school. The dogs go through rigorous training sessions like Rin Tin Tin or canine units with the police academy. This would be the answer.

We located a reputable puppy school, Kennelwise Canine Obedience School, near our apartment. The classes were held once a week for eight weeks. There were strict requirements, including the expectation that the masters be present for each session. It should have dawned on me with this requirement that canine obedience training wasn't completely about the dog; the master may need some training, too.

We arrived with Allie's Kennelwise application papers in hand. We were excited to get started and arrived early. We weren't the only ones; the other students were already there. Allie's class consisted of eight dogs. Six were first-time students, and two dogs were repeat students. I couldn't help feeling sorry for those lower-functioning pupils who had flunked the basic obedience course. I had confidence in Allie to do better.

The class was a broad spectrum of breeds. There were a Collie, a Yorkie, a Poodle, a Labrador, a Scottie, a German Shepherd, a Cocker Spaniel, and our Bichon. All the dogs were over six months old but less than two years of age. Each dog and its master seemed pleasant and ordinary . . . except for one. There's always one. The Cocker Spaniel strutted around like only a Cocker can. I've often wondered if the breed has been misnamed and should more aptly have been called "Cocky Spaniel"?

This beautiful dog had the gait and air of pedigree. She obviously came from good blood and pure breeding. Her full registered name, Princess Tava, fit her nobility. But even more than the presence of this Cocker Spaniel was the confidence of her owners, a young, well-dressed couple. The crest embroidered on the husband's sweater was the family coat of arms. The three of them huddled together, whispering private conversations. I couldn't help wondering what they were saying as they glanced towards Allie who trotted happily at my side. Their expression was one of disdain and contempt.

"We should feel good about who Allie is rubbing paws with," I jokingly told Tracy.

At seven P.M. on the nose, the instructor walked into the room. "Good evening, class. Welcome to Kennelwise." She smiled broadly. "We have been in the business of obedience training for dogs since 1972. I think you will have a good experience. Our program is tough, strict and demanding but worthwhile. Let's get down to business."

I found myself sizing up the competition. Yep, you can take 'em, Allie. Did the other owners have similar thoughts?

The instructor continued. "I want you to line up largest dog to smallest, right to left. This will be your assigned order for the next eight weeks. I would like each of you in your place so we can start promptly at seven. Tonight we will be working on one of the most basic but essential commands a pet and his master need to conquer. Although the easiest concept, this may be the greatest challenge. This is where the master begins to gain an advantage over the pet's will."

"Did you hear that Allie?" I asked.

Allie glanced up at the sound of my voice only to give me a dismissive look.

There were two masters with each pet. We were given a handful of doggie treats made of liver. Allie had not yet met a food she disliked, and the liver treats were no exception. One master would go to the other end of the room about ten feet away, while the second master remained with the pet. Upon the teacher's command, each pet was released. The master across the room called out the pet's name excitedly and encouraged the pet to come to him.

With the exception of Allie, at first the dogs went in every direction. Some stayed with their masters and some played with other dogs. The dogs stopped to smell the ground where other canines before them had deposited their unique odor. When each dog was finally coaxed across the room, the master gave it a treat.

Allie was the only dog who ran straight from Tracy to me upon command. This will be a breeze, I thought, and praised Allie for her obedience.

We repeated this exercise several times with similar outcomes. By around the fourth pass, all the dogs had begun to go directly from one master to the other. Now the instructor asked us to back up two feet. We did this for several more passes until our pet conquered the twenty-foot distance. It was entertaining.

I looked around at the other owners and dogs. The Labrador's parents looked and dressed liked hunters. The Lab instinctively ran from one master to the next as if he were tracking down a wounded pheasant. The Cocker Spaniel and her parents continued to attract my attention. The Cocker princess would huddle next to her master while the parent across the room stated in a confident tone, "Come here, Princess." While I observed these three, I couldn't help thinking of some duke and duchess in an aristocratic land bespeaking, "Come thou hither, Princess Tava."

I caught myself looking with disdain at how confident they appeared. Princess would tiptoe, then prance over to her master in a manner that begged the question, "Do I have to walk on this grimy floor? I might get my paws dirty." In the meantime, the other dogs ignored them. In a canine world, prestige and influence mean little.

Our next task was to walk with our pet on a lead. The master was to walk with the lead in the left hand and the pet on the left side. We were to walk our dog in a big circle around the room, staying three to four steps behind the dog in front of us. When the instructor said, "Stop" or "Heel," the owner was to pull on the lead, restraining the pet at his side. When the instructor said "Lead," we were to walk counter-clockwise around the room. Allie and Tracy would start, then I would change out with Tracy. We were assigned a place behind the Cocker Spaniel.

The Cocker was already skilled at leading. She tossed her head back and pointed her nose in the air, arched her back and strutted around the room.

When it was her turn, however, Allie simply plopped her rump on the floor with her two hind legs sticking straight out in front. Tracy said, "Come on, Allie, get up. Let's go," and tugged at the lead. Allie dug in.

After nearly a minute of coaxing and holding up the dogs in line behind us, the instructor stepped in. "Class, stop for a moment. This is a good example of how your will and your dog's will don't always coincide. You will notice how the little Bichon has decided she doesn't wish to lead. Let me show you what to do when this happens. May I?"

She took the leash from Tracy. "What you do is take out any slack in the leash and then proceed to force the dog into obedience, gently but forcefully. The floor is slick, so you may have to drag the dog gently alongside you for a few steps until she gets the idea that you are the master."

Allie pinned her ears back in defiance as the instructor began to slide her around the room on her rump.

The instructor continued to speak as she demonstrated. "She'll get the hang of it." But the more the instructor spoke, the more determined Allie became.

"If you just keep at it, eventually she'll comply," the instructor said, reassuringly. The tone in her voice grew firmer with each word. Halfway around the room, with Allie still in tow like a water skier behind a speedboat, the instructor became visibly irritated.

"Sometimes you have to stop and pick her hind quarters off the ground and force her to stand, then proceed." She reached down and picked Allie up to a standing position, then began to lead again. Like a rag doll, Allie's hind legs went limp and she flopped on the ground.

The other dog owners began to laugh, and the instructor grew red in the face. "I've never had a dog slide all the way around the room before," she said defensively. There was a hesitance in her voice. It almost sounded as if she were stating the rules of engagement.

Even the dogs appeared to be laughing at this formal display of disobedience, all except one. The Cocker Spaniel again had that look of disgust on her face. The parents seemed equally annoyed.

For a moment it seemed as if the class had begun to root for Allie, as if the underdog had challenged the head trainer to a tug-of-war. I could feel the class cheering for Allie to slide around the entire room.

Upon turning the final corner, the instructor pulled on the leash. Allie again pinned her ears back stronger than a stubborn mule. The instructor stopped one step short of the complete lap around the room, handed the lead to Tracy, and muttered, "You try."

I was as surprised as anyone. The instructor stole a victory from our precious Allie. For a split second, I was annoyed.

At the handoff of the leash, Allie immediately hopped up and began to walk along Tracy's right side, head high, nearly prancing. Obviously, in reaction to the trainer, Allie thought, "You're not my mom!" My irritation with Allie quickly vanished with the realization that she had once again established the levels of authority. She was in charge!

The parade around the room resumed in a more orderly fashion with the uppity Cocker Spaniel a few strides ahead of Allie. With much of the class still focused on Allie, she placed an exclamation point upon her disobedient act. She raced up behind the high-tuned Cocker Spaniel planted her black, cold, wet, nose right behind the Spaniel's tail, and goosed her. The Cocker darted forward, tail between her legs.

"Can't you control your dog?" A sharp voice rose above all others in the room. Princess Tava's Mom could not restrain herself.

"Oh, excuse us," Tracy said smiling.

Allie was compliant for the few remaining minutes in class. She pranced along Tracy's side one full lap around the room with her mouth open, tongue lolling, and an expression of glee upon her face.

The battleline had been drawn. Each week we found a natural foe in the Cocker Spaniel and her parents. Yet the other dogs and owners remained focused on themselves and the natural challenges associated with canine obedience school.

Over the weeks, Allie learned to lead. And she rolled over and learned to sit. Our hunch was that Allie liked liver treats so much, she would do anything for them. Some tasks she mastered, while others she did reluctantly. As pupils go, she was wavering between a C and a D simply because she remained a free spirit. Our bond with her tightened, however; our appreciation and respect for one another grew as we completed our puppy and master training. We were proud of her bold and independent spirit.

We showed off Allie's new skills to friends and family. Sometimes she pulled her ears back and gave us that defiant look, but usually if she received some type of edible reward, she complied, however reluctantly.

The final week before graduation we were to bring in our pet's kennel. The instructor preached the value and importance of each pet having a home crate, kennel, or bed, to become familiar with as its home. Pets respond to having a safe, secure place where they can stay when left home alone, the teacher explained.

Each set of owners arrived with their pet and kennel in hand. As predicted, the Cocker Spaniel family arrived with a frou-frou, fluffy bed with sequins along the sides.

"Tonight we will be ending our class with assisting your pet in getting into its kennel or bed upon command. Here is the technique: One master holds the pet while the other places a liver treat in the kennel and says, 'into your cage.' The second master then releases the pet and observes that the pet goes into its crate."

This appeared simple and logical. With a liver treat involved, I was confident that Allie could handle this task.

Princess Tava caught my eye. She was perched atop her fancy bed in a manner suited for nobility. The only thing missing was a tiara. The woman picked Princess Tava carefully out of her bed, and the fellow owner positioned himself over the bed with treat in hand.

We awaited the instructor's final commands. "Before we begin, let me say what a pleasure it has been having each of you in our class. I've enjoyed getting to know you and assisting you with your precious pet. Maybe we'll see one of you at the American Kennel Club or Westminster Dog Show some day," the instructor concluded.

 While she spoke, I had relaxed my grip on Allie's leash. Before I realized it, Allie pulled the leash from my hand and trotted toward the edge of the room. Her being loose initially startled the class, then a hush fell over the crowd.

Visibly irritated by Allie, the instructor stopped in the middle of her closing remarks, and with the authority of a law-enforcement officer she stated, "Restrain your dog! Please restrain your dog!"

A split second later, Allie made her final declaration of independence as she bounded on top of Princess Tava's noble bed, squatted and pottied.

Around the room were blank stares and mouths agape. We stood in stunned silence. Allie finished her duty, then trotted back and sat down beside me.

I glanced nervously around the room—all eyes were on Allie. After what seemed an eternity, a few chuckles broke out and pierced the silence. Then the room erupted in laughter.

At that moment, it dawned on me; Allie had calculated the precise moment to pull off this act of disobedience. She had been waiting for this opportunity for eight weeks. At first I was embarrassed and ashamed, but upon further reflection, I realized I was proud of her.

I hadn't liked the couple's attitude from the moment I saw them. They seemed to look down on the rest of us. Even though I couldn't condone Allie's behavior, I was pleased inside. I probably wouldn't have chosen to express myself in this fashion, but Allie's action said even more effectively what I was thinking. I patted her head affectionately.

Against all odds, Allie did receive her doggy school diploma. We were now the proud parents of a full-fledged American Kennel Club-trained Bichon Frise. She hadn't been the star pupil, but she made the experience mighty exciting.

Yet, we wondered who had really received the obedience training— Did we train the dog or was the dog training us?

CHAPTER 4

Hide the Shoes: *Overcoming Obsessive Chewing Disorder*

Having successfully completed puppy obedience training, we still had a few behavioral issues to overcome. Allie, well over a year old by now, continued her OCD, Obsessive Chewing Disorder. Although I had yet to see a diagnostic medical code for this mental illness, her actions told me there must be one.

"Maybe it's because of her teething," I said, trying to reassure Tracy.

"But she lost her last baby tooth six months ago," Tracy countered.

We consulted the Kennelwise instructor, and she gave sound advice. "Fill a spray bottle with water, and every time Allie chews on something, give her a squirt. If that doesn't work, try a spurt of lemon juice directly in her mouth."

We watched Allie closely and when she began to chew on the furniture, we squirted her with water. At first, it startled her, but then she seemed to enjoy the whole experience. With each squirt, she stopped chewing and tried to catch the stream in her mouth. I tried setting the nozzle on full blast, then sneaked up behind her and sprayed a full stream of water on her backside. She jumped up surprised, then darted about, trying to catch a mouthful of water. In the meantime, this neat little game had no effect on her excessive chewing.

"Let's try the lemon juice," Tracy suggested. So we picked up a small, yellow, lemon-shaped bottle from the store. We intended to mix it with water, but decided if diluted lemon juice would work, straight lemon concentrate would be even better.

We waited. The next time Allie started to chew on some forbidden object, Tracy got out the lemon juice and placed the bottle next to Allie's mouth. With one giant squeeze, Allie's mouth was filled with lip-puckering juice. She sat stunned for a moment, then began to gyrate. She desperately licked and gasped, then ran over and lapped up most of the water in her bowl to rid her taste buds of that foul experience.

It wasn't long before Allie chewed on one of our shoes. Tracy took the lemon-juice bottle out of the refrigerator and headed toward Allie. Allie immediately looked up from the shoe. Her eyes locked onto the bottle, and she twitched uncomfortably. As Tracy moved the bottle up toward Allie, she raised her gums, showing her teeth. Tracy moved the bottle away and Allie relaxed her sneer. Tracy brought the bottle toward Allie, and Allie's lips curled under. Again, she exposed her teeth and gums. She was growling without sound.

Finally, we had something to get her attention. Sure enough, with only one more squirt, we were able to cure her OCD. (Over the years, lemon juice continued to be the only thing that got Allie's attention with regard to discipline or obedience.)

Soon an unusual behavior caught our attention that turned out to be more natural than we first realized. One afternoon after wrestling Allie through a bath, we struggled to catch her and dry her off. She darted about the apartment like the Energizer bunny on amphetamines. She raced around the room, between the furniture, into the bedroom, and back out again. This went on for several minutes, with her showing no signs of tiring.

Then abruptly, in midstride, she stopped, sat smack down on the ground with her lower legs stretched in front of her. She then proceeded to use her two front legs to pull herself along the floor, dragging her bottom on the carpet. It had been years since I'd read James Herriot's *All Creatures Great and Small*, but a single neuron fired in the deep crevices of my brain. I recognized this behavior. Mr. Herriot, a veterinarian in England, described Tricky Woo, a Pekingese, who often went "flop-bott," but I couldn't recall why Tricky Woo had done this.

After some research, I found this behavior was due to impacted anal glands. I'd never heard or seen this behavior in human medicine, but then again, why would I? What person would drag himself across the floor to scratch his bottom?

This behavior became more frequent in Allie. After a veterinary consultation with my dad, we learned that Allie needed her anal glands expressed. We had not realized that the Bichon Frise breed had common issues with anal glands. To make light of a potentially embarrass- ing situation, we Americanized the term as "going flop-bottom," and over the years kept track of the longest distance Allie dragged herself along the ground. I think ten feet was her record.

Bichons are occasionally described as lovable clowns who desire to entertain their owner. Before we knew the real reason, we wondered if Allie's flop-bottom antics were her attempt to amuse Tracy and me.

On more than one occasion, I wondered if Allie actually had the mind of a human. Since I had failed to recognize her body language, she resorted to a more desperate method of communication. She went flop-bottom as her own way to alert me her anal glands needed expressing.

One afternoon she uncharacteristically followed me around the apartment, whining and whimpering. When I failed to understand her, she disappeared.

"Where did Allie go?" I asked Tracy.

"I don't know."

I went from room to room looking for her. Finally, I found her in the bathroom, sitting in the bathtub.

"What are you doing in there?" I asked her. Our eyes met. She was trying to speak to me. "What is it?" I asked.

I was reminded of the old sitcom "Lassie." Lassie was extremely protective of her young owner, a boy named Timmy. Unlike Timmy, who knew full well that Lassie would instinctively lead a search party to where he had fallen down a well, I was less adept when it came to understanding Allie's communication. Like Timmy being pulled from the well, similarly I lifted Allie out of the tub and sat her on the bathroom tile.

She stared at me with her dark, expressive eyes, then jumped back into the tub. At this moment it dawned on me—perhaps she wanted her anal glands expressed. I grabbed some tissues and performed the delicate, yet invasive procedure. Immediately, Allie's expression changed to happy-go-lucky. She hopped out of the tub and pranced out of the bathroom.

Allie had once again trained me, the so-called master, to perform yet another act of obedience.

CHAPTER 5

Allie Unleashed: *Lost and Thankfully Found*

I decided to change my direction in medicine from radiology to family practice. I interviewed for a family medicine residency spot at Truman East Medical Center in Kansas City, Missouri. The interview went well, and I was offered the internship. We would be moving from St. Louis, where Tracy was born and raised, to Kansas City.

Allie took change in stride. Tracy had a harder time. So when my career path took a different turn, I was mighty glad to have Allie providing extra love and support for Tracy. My decision to get Tracy a companion proved wise.

Seeing Tracy's loneliness after the move, I began to wonder if I had made the right decision. Yet, Allie remained a steady constant in our lives. Her routine remained the same. The consistency of her schedule provided a source of familiarity and, in turn comfort, for Tracy. Allie's demeanor was unwavering. She appeared unflappable. Tracy and I both appreciated Allie's willingness to accept change without any fuss. She remained generally excited about another opportunity to enjoy each day.

I could learn a lot from her, and when I stopped and listened, I did. Frequently, I'd be running late in the morning, yet this was the time Allie demanded my attention. Just as I was about to race off to work, I saw Allie by the door, her signal to me that she wanted a walk. More times than not, I brushed her request off. However, the rare times when I agreed, the walk proved more beneficial to me than to her. Without fail, when I made the time for a five-minute jaunt with Allie through the neighborhood, I always returned more relaxed and less stressed. I came to understand: Allie loved the walk—I needed it.

We purchased our first home in Lee's Summit, Missouri, a suburb on the east side of Kansas City. Our neighborhood was a new subdivision with home construction on all sides. The backyard was not yet fenced in, so for Allie's sake, we put up a makeshift fence until we could build our own.

But several times Allie found a way of escape. Even though she never wandered far, her running off concerned me. She was not street smart. She could get hit by a car. Preoccupied with worry, I spent the next few months building a basic fence around our backyard.

The neighbor to the east of us was an ER doctor, a divorced woman with two girls and four-legged Madonna, an oversized potbelly pig. Madonna was an outdoor pig, who occupied their fenced-in backyard. From the looks of things, Madonna ruled the sty.

Every morning Allie approached the fence cautiously, sniffing and smelling. When least expected, she would bark loudly and incessantly. Since puppy school, she had been assertive, and I frequently wondered if she would be an alpha female in a pack of wild dogs.

One afternoon the neighbors asked if Tracy and I would like to meet their potbelly pig.

"Sure, bring Madonna over," I said. Like Allie, I was curious to meet this creature.

In a matter of minutes, the front doorbell rang. There on our stoop were our neighbors. Standing next to them was their pet pig. She wore a harness rather than a collar and was restrained by a leash.

Would that lead hold a hefty animal like this? I wondered.

Madonna was more assertive than Allie. On their first visit, the pig charged her, as if to say hello, swine style. Allie yelped, placed her tail between her legs, and darted away. This surprised me. She had sounded so tough barking through the fence. In Allie's defense, Madonna was mighty frightening. She was even larger than she appeared through the fence. I guessed she weighed at least eighty-five pounds. Her entire body was covered in wiry hair. Her snout was huge and wrinkled in and out as she sniffed the air. Maybe Madonna was an alpha pig?

Over time, Allie befriended Madonna. Allie would snoot and root around in the dirt and then grunt as if she were a pig. How had she developed the ability to make this noise? One of the characteristics of Bichons is digging through dirt, rooting out rodents from their hole. In Lee's Summit, Allie perfected this behavior, which raised a question: had she been digging instinctively, or had Madonna shown her the ropes of a pig's life?

Allie and Madonna played a game where Madonna would push her snout under the fence, and Allie tried to touch noses before Madonna squealed and ran away. They repeated the process like two children playing tag.

The fenced-in backyard restrained Allie nicely, and she had a new friend, albeit a pig. Tracy had adapted fairly well. My work hours were often long, and Allie again provided companionship. After four months, we were settled into our new life.

One weekend Tracy's parents and twenty-eight-year-old brother Shawn, who had Down's syndrome, came for a visit. They arrived Friday night, and we spent that evening and Saturday enjoying each other's company and showing them the town. Because this was their first official visit to our new home, we made dinner reservations at a landmark four-star restaurant in downtown Kansas City.

Around three in the afternoon Tracy announced we had to leave at five-fifteen for a six o'clock dinner reservation.

I came in from outside and asked Tracy, "Where's Allie?"

"I don't know."

We casually looked around our split-level house. Allie was nowhere to be found. On the ground floor, the door to the garage had a touchy handle that often failed to latch completely. I noticed that the door was partly open; besides, we had left the garage door open about six inches.

"Tracy, I'm afraid she's outside," I concluded. Tracy agreed.

We opened the garage door fully and extended our search. I headed out on foot, and Tracy and her mom got into the car and cased the neighborhood. Shawn and John, Tracy's father, stayed at home in case Allie returned on her own.

She couldn't be too far, I tried to convince myself, picking up my pace.

We searched for forty-five minutes before we met at home to regroup.

"Have you spoken to the neighbors?" Tracy asked.

"Not yet. Great idea."

We went next door to Madonna's house. They hadn't seen Allie, but offered to help us look for Allie. Terrible thoughts raced through my mind. Could she have been stolen? Had someone invited her into their house and was claiming her as his own? Had she gotten hit by a car? Was she scared and wandering around not knowing which way to run? We resumed our search with a larger search party

It was now approaching four thirty in the afternoon. If we didn't find her soon, we would either have to cancel our reservations or postpone our search. I began to panic. What would life be like without Allie? She was as important as any member of our family. Should I put up lost-dog signs with Allie's picture around town? Would the police assist us with our search? Should I notify the pound and see if any lost dog has been brought in? My obsessive listing of fearful questions made me feel even worse.

At four forty-five we met back at the house again to plan our next strategy and make a decision about dinner. We were gathered in the kitchen, agonizing, while Tracy stood at the sink. As she washed her hands, she stared blankly out the kitchen window. Just then something caught her eye.

Without saying a word, she ran to the back door and squinted at the dirt pile behind our house, on the lot where new home construction had begun. The mound was three hundred feet—the length of a football field-from our back deck.

"I think that's Allie!" She shrieked, then raced down the stairs with us chasing behind. She ran along our fence, then bolted through the gate and headed toward the huge pile of dirt. The earthmovers had been digging a hole for the basement of a new home. The displaced dirt formed a six-foot-tall and fifteen-foot-wide mound.

Sure enough, perched atop the pile of dirt was a filthy ball of fur and mud. Allie's white coat was soiled and black. The fur around her nose was caked with mud, and clumps of clay hung from her ears, her paws, and her legs.

Tracy retrieved Allie from the mud and hugged her. She looked as if she had been rolling around the muddy dirt pile like a pig wallows in his sty or manure pile. Come to think of it, she looked like Madonna. Had Madonna taught Allie some of the sacred ways of swine? Maybe we'd hear of Madonna barking or going flop-bottom one of these days.

We had located our precious pooch in the nick of time. It wasn't too late to keep our dinner reservations.

After a wonderful evening on the town, I believed it was only appropriate to ask for a "doggy bag." We had a big scare that day. The mere thought of losing Allie made me appreciate her even more. A special dog like her deserved a succulent piece of K.C. strip from a four-star restaurant.

I reflected upon the events of the afternoon on our drive home. We must be more careful in the future, I gently reprimanded all of us. Allie was so young then, only two. We still had many wonderful years left with her.

CHAPTER 6

Operation Allie: *A One-Night Kennel Stand*

My dad was nearing retirement from practicing vet medicine, and I thought it a good opportunity to have Allie spayed. She was almost a year old. Dad knew money was tight while I was a resident in training, and he was more than willing to help us out. We planned a Memorial Day weekend trek from Kansas City to see my folks in Colby.

Whenever we went anywhere, we always brought Allie along. We treated her like a furry little person. Between us in the front seat of our car, Allie sat upon a posh seat like a queen sits on her throne, for whatever journey lie ahead.

My dad never saw eye-to-eye with Tracy about Allie traveling with us. He had irritated Tracy on more than one occasion with snide remarks about keeping a dog in its place. She had exercised restraint in not giving him a piece of her mind, but the facial expressions she reserved for his derogatory comments about Allie and traveling spoke more than a thousand words.

During this trip back home, we decided to travel with my parents to

Garden City, Kansas, to see my maternal grandparents. My dad's folks had already passed away. Grandpa and Grandma were both in their late eighties, and I believed we should try and see them whenever possible.

Saturday morning we were to leave around nine o'clock for the two-hour drive south to my grandparents. Tracy made it clear we would be taking Allie with us. She was not going to leave Allie at my folks' home, penned up in a cage for what could easily be ten to twelve hours. This was not negotiable.

Having to tell my dad about this decision was not something I was thrilled about, but I had a responsibility to Tracy and Allie. My parents still had great influence over me. The last thing I wanted was a confrontation followed by a two-hour car ride.

Around eight-thirty in the morning I approached my dad. "Allie's coming with us to Garden City."

"What?"

I tried a softer approach. "You know Grandpa and Grandma love dogs, and I want them to see Allie."

"Kipp, I don't like that one bit. Why would you drag a dog with you? You know . . ."

In my head I finished with the words I had heard most of my life: A dog should know his place is at home. Who's the master, and who's the dog?

The discussion turned into a full-fledged argument that ended with my saying to the man I had respected and feared all of my life, "It's either all three of us or none of us. That's how it's going to be."

Nothing more was said.

At a couple minutes to nine, Allie, Tracy, and I—with Allie's cage placed in the trunk—climbed into the backseat of my parents' car. Allie was lying on a pillow between Tracy and me. Mom and Dad slid into the front, and we traveled in silence for the first thirty minutes or so. The tension in the car was palpable.

Mom let us stew in frigid silence for a while and then broke the ice. "Let's play a game."

"Okay!" I quickly chimed in.

"I don't know if any of you have played this game before," Mother continued. "Each of us starts with five toothpicks. The object is to get all twenty toothpicks (and the other players having none.) It's called 'I Never.' You think of something that you know other people probably have done but you haven't. For example, I say I never attended Franklin High School. Since your father did go to Franklin High School, he gives me a toothpick. Because you and Tracy didn't attend Franklin High School, you don't gain or lose a toothpick."

"Okay, sounds easy enough," I said.

Tracy agreed. Dad drove in continued silence.

Mom handed out five toothpicks to each one of us. "Kipp, you start. You get thirty seconds to come up with your statement, or you forfeit your turn."

"I've got one," I said. "I never flew an airplane."

Both Mom and Dad had piloted their own single-engine plane years before, so each of them handed over a toothpick. Tracy kept hers.

"Tracy, your turn," Mom stated.

"OK. I was never born in Kansas." This time, Mom and I each surrendered a toothpick to Tracy.

"Dad was born in Nebraska." I interjected, saving Tracy from having to ask Dad for a toothpick.

"I'll go next," Mom said. "I've never lived in Missouri."

Tracy and I each gave her a toothpick.

"Your turn, Dad," I said. No response.

"Vic, it's your turn," Mom coaxed.

"Okay, Dad," I continued. "The clock's ticking. You have thirty seconds."

We sat in silence for twenty-five seconds.

Then Dad spoke firmly and succinctly. "I never let a damn dog rule my life."

We sat stunned, then I burst out laughing. So did Mom.

Finally, Tracy began to laugh.

"Oh, yeah? What about Snookie?" I asked. Babee Snookums was their Poodle, and she had replaced us kids when we left home.

In typical Allie fashion, she somehow sensed she was the center of the discussion. She hopped up, jumped between the armrests to the front seat, then crawled on to Dad's lap and sat there staring up at him. Dad smiled. The game resumed, and our trip was pleasant for the remainder of the day. We arrived home late that Saturday evening.

Dad made fewer and fewer comments about the privileges we afforded our Allie. I know it always bugged him, but he learned to keep it to himself.

On Sunday, Dad and I took Allie to the clinic early in the morning. She was not happy. I hadn't fed her, and she couldn't understand why. Around seven thirty, we prepped Allie for surgery.

My dad had practiced vet medicine about thirty years. I have no idea how many hysterectomies he had done, but it must be in the thousands. He was a strong proponent of having a female dog's uterus and ovaries removed at a fairly young age, provided the dog was not to be used for breeding. Small dogs were at greater risk for mammary cancer—the equivalent of breast cancer in humans—and having a hysterectomy at a young age prevented problems.

Tracy and I had decided that Allie would not have puppies. The added work would be too much, and more important, we would not be able to give up the puppies. With our luck, Allie would have a half dozen in her litter. We didn't want a houseful of dogs. I had mixed feelings about this decision but knew it was for the best.

Dad administered the anesthesia, and the surgery was soon underway. It didn't take long to perform the procedure, about thirty minutes from start to finish.

I had assisted my dad many times over the years, but this was the first time since I had completed medical school. My recent experiences in medicine had given me an entirely new respect and appreciation for my father's skills, both as a clinician and as a surgeon. The skill with which he performed this routine, but delicate surgery on an animal whose anatomy was significantly smaller than that of a human being impressed me even more. I was preoccupied with these thoughts throughout Allie's surgery.

In what seemed like only minutes, Dad completed the operation and closed the skin. Just as he placed the last suture, Allie began to stir.

"Calculated that dose just right," Dad said, pleased.

We placed a small dressing on Allie's surgical wound and placed a funnel-shaped (Elizabethan) collar around her neck. I observed her for several minutes until Dad completed some paperwork. When she had nearly awakened, I placed her on a towel and carried her to the car.

At home she dozed on and off for about one hour, then showed some signs of pain and overall lethargy.

By early Monday morning she was better, and we felt we could make our trip home. Allie slept most of the way. When we completed our seven-hour journey across Kansas, it was nearly nine P.M. I was scheduled to work in the morning. Tracy would be off.

Upon arriving home, I gently lifted Allie from the car and carried her inside. While she lay in my arms, I noticed the bandages around her abdomen were partly red. This disturbed me. Upon closer inspection, I detected blood-tinged fluid along her incision. Besides, she was running a fever.

I called Dad. "Should I give her a baby aspirin?" I asked.

"Shouldn't hurt," he replied.

"Should we be concerned?"

"Probably not," he said. "Just keep an eye on her."

Around midnight, I woke up to find Allie and Tracy awake. Allie was violently sick. She had vomited nonstop for thirty minutes. I called an emergency veterinary service and explained Allie's recent surgery and her current condition.

"Bring her up," the voice on the line suggested.

We arrived at the clinic around three thirty A.M. and stayed until five. The vet started an IV and began to fill Allie with fluids.

"She's dehydrated," he said. "She also has a low-grade fever. Come back around eight."

When Tracy and I came back at eight, the vet said Allie was not much better.

"How serious is this?" I asked.

"It seems rather serious because we can't determine what's causing her fever. Did anything unusual happen during her surgery?"

"Nothing at all," I replied.

"Maybe it's the aspirin," the vet suggested.

"Really?" I asked, puzzled. "It was a baby aspirin."

"Might be that, plus a combination of mild infection," he stated. "I want to keep her all day and possibly tonight."

"I can't let her stay here all day and then all night, too," Tracy said.

"I want to do everything I can to see that she survives," the vet said sternly.

"Tracy, if this is what's best, we have to do it," I said.

"Can I come up and see her?" Tracy asked.

"Yes, you can see her now, again at one, then come back around five, and we'll decide if she has to stay overnight."

Allie looked vulnerable and frail. Her eyes were listless; she had hardly any energy, but her tail wagged as we entered the room. There were five steel cages, two on the bottom and three on the top. Allie was in the top cage, about waist height. Two other dogs and a cat were convalescing in the other cages. The room was clean but sterile, dark but calm. Tracy began to cry. Tears welled up in my eyes, too.

"You have to get better, Allie," Tracy said. "I don't know what I'd do without you." Allie licked Tracy's hand as if to console her.

After about twenty minutes, the vet said we had to leave. I headed off to work, and Tracy went home. When she returned to the clinic promptly at one P.M., she called me and said Allie was about the same.

When I got off at four thirty, I picked Tracy up at home, and we went directly to the animal hospital. The vet and his staff were expecting us. We ventured in to see Allie, then spoke with the doctor.

"Her labs are getting better, but I really think she should stay overnight." His words had a sharp bite.

"Are you sure?" I asked.

"Yes."

Tracy broke down. After a lengthy good-bye, we left Allie to spend her first ever night away from home in a kennel.

The time passed slowly. I tried to reassure Tracy. I even tried to get her to go out to eat or to see a movie. She wanted no part of either.

The vet was kind to call us around nine P.M. and give us an update. The news was encouraging. "She's really perked up," he said.

"Can we come and get her?" Tracy asked.

"No, she needs to stay, but I think she can go home tomorrow."

After a sleepless night, we headed to the clinic at seven thirty. True to his word, the doctor released Allie to our care. She was given some strict dietary and specific fluid-intake instructions. She seemed herself when we drove home, happy to be back in the presence of her humans. We decided the culprit must have been the baby aspirin.

Tracy never lost another battle with regard to Allie staying a night in a kennel. Had we been playing "I Never," Allie could have said, "I never spent a second night in a kennel, and I never had another aspirin in my life." And it would have been worth two toothpicks.

Chapter 7

The Look-Alike Grandfather: *Meeting the People of Weston and Their Dogs*

I graduated from family medicine residency and took a job an hour's drive from Lee's Summit, in Weston, Missouri, a small town north of Kansas City. The 1992 housing market offered "slim pickins," but after several house-hunting trips, we finally settled for an antebellum "fixer-upper."

When we pulled out of our driveway in Lee's Summit, Tracy was tearful. Our time there had been thoroughly enjoyable. Our house was brand new, nothing fancy but more than enough for a young couple's starter home.

When we arrived at our destination, one of the movers pulled Tracy aside and said, "Now I can understand why you were so distraught, leaving your nice home for this one here." The house needed a lot of work, but I could see beyond the red shag carpet and the boxed-in floor plan.

We hired a local carpenter named Benny. During the day I began building a medical practice in our new clinic, which had been built by my new employer and sponsoring hospital. At the same time, Tracy and I spent our spare time, and all our spare money, rebuilding our home from the ground up. It was exciting to see our house taking shape. The remodeling, though expensive, was necessary and thrilling.

Allie took all this in stride. Each day presented her with two square meals, multiple treats and a collection of new adventures.

When we moved in, our yard was not fenced. I immediately cut down the fifteen or more trees behind our house, and for weeks I sawed and stacked logs. Then I began work on the fence. Recalling the problems I encountered with our fence in Lee's Summit, I realized I was an amateur fence builder. So, I sought the advice of my brother, Kurt, an all-around handy man. He affectionately named us the Two Stooges' Fence Company.

One Saturday I rented the one-man gas-operated post hole digger. I had marked all thirty-five post sites the night before, hoping to be able to finish digging all thirty-five of them by sundown the next day—a BHAG (Big Hairy Audacious Goal)! I arrived at the rental shop early, eager to get started.

Around eight thirty, I broke the Saturday morning peace and quiet in our neighborhood by revving up the auger. I placed the large drill-bit auger over the first hole along the backside of the house. After revving the motor, I pushed the corkscrew drill bit into the ground. In seconds, I buried it to the brim. Where's the reverse, I thought?

About that time, our neighbor, Tom Pendergrast, came strolling by. He always wore overalls and a T-shirt. "Got her buried, eh?" He asked. Mr. Pendergrast had been a mail carrier for years, but was now retired.

"Yes, and I can't figure out where the reverse is."

Mr. Pendergrast chuckled. "No reverse?"

"Yep, that's right. I can't find the reverse."

"That's right," he restated. "No reverse."

His repeating my statements was irritating me. I could feel the flush upon my face. "Well, you can see I buried the auger, and now I want to get it out of the ground. I'm trying to find the reverse."

"Sure enough," he said with a twinkle in his eyes. "You buried it all right. No reverse."

He had worn me down. After a few more seconds of searching the machine for the reverse switch, I asked directly, "Mr. Pendergrast, can you show me where the reverse switch is located?"

"That's what I've been trying to tell you. There is no reverse!"

He was right. There was no reverse. The auger, when used properly, didn't need a reverse. Mr. Pendergrast headed on down the road. I could hear him chuckling out loud. My ignorance regarding the auger embarrassed me. It was clear that at least one neighbor was entertained by my mishap. I waited for his figure to blend into the horizon, hoping that I could rectify my mistake before any other neighbors so the auger buried deep into the ground. When the coast was clear, I returned with a spade and spent the next hour shoveling out the posthole digger. It would have been easier by hand, I thought.

Building the fence became a several months' long project, consuming most of my free time. Before the fence was completed, Allie had become very finicky. It got to the point where we were unable to find the perfect spot for her to empty her colon and bladder around the neighborhood.

One evening I was working late at the clinic catching up on paperwork when I heard a familiar jingle. Allie stood in my doorway. She cocked her head and stared intently at me.

"Well, what are you doing up here?" I asked. She approached my outstretched hand, licked it and then sniffed around the clinic. The carpet was filled with all types of strange and unusual smells, which she relished. By now Tracy had come around the corner.

"What are you two doing here?" I asked.

"She wouldn't potty or poo poo," there was disgust in Tracy's voice. "We made three trips around the block. Every time she acted like she had located just the right spot, some sound or smell distracted her. The little cuss, she can be so irritating sometimes. So I brought her here!"

"Any luck?"

"Sure. As soon as we got here, she hopped out of the car, trotted behind the evergreen tree and relieved herself. I can't wait till we get that fence completed!"

Her reminder seared my conscience. "You're right. I need to get it done."

Over the next months, Benny completed the deck on the back of our house. My brother and I spent the rest of the summer and most of the fall completing the fence so Allie could have her own backyard. We had begun to call the house the "money pit." All of our extra money went towards remodeling. Several times I was tempted to hire someone to finish the fence, but I knew the money would be better spent elsewhere. That, and the fact that I couldn't let someone else finish something that I started. The idea that anyone should personally finish anything they started was deeply embedded in my brain, something mom and dad had demanded of me and my siblings, growing up.

In the meantime, we put Allie's obedience training to use and led her around the neighborhood. Soon this became a routine. She was a creature of habit and liked the jaunt around the block. Only inclement weather gave Tracy or me a reprieve, as this was the only time when Allie got right down to business. Amazingly, in the rain Allie instantly located the right spot, promptly did her business, then darted inside.

Usually, we conned our guests into assisting us with Allie's twice-daily constitutionals. We used every tactic we could think of, including guilt. My tactics approached ruthlessness. "Don't you want to help raise your adorable, furry, granddaughter?" Or, "She seems to be happiest when you walk her. I don't know what it is, she obviously prefers you. You must be her favorite!" Of course, this worked only a couple of times before our guests read through my deviousness and graciously but sternly declined.

Every morning around six thirty, Allie went out front. She stayed within the front yard, probably because she knew her breakfast was waiting inside. But every evening her internal alarm tolled six bells at six when she insisted upon her second meal of the day and the stroll that followed.

Soon all of the neighbors knew us by name. Many times she refused to potty the first trip around, forcing us to travel a second time around the block. She had a knack for knowing when we were in a hurry—these were usually the times she needed a second pass.

In predictable, willful fashion, Allie broke many of the puppy training rules and tugged on the lead. Even though she weighed only around fifteen pounds, she had the strength to drag us along.

One night when Dad was visiting, he reluctantly consented to taking his four-legged granddaughter on her walk—after all, he did want to be a positive influence in her life.

After we opened the door, Allie charged out, jerking Dad, armed with pooper scooper, in tow. The walk—more like a trot—had started as usual. Allie tugged on the leash, and Dad gently pulled back. Occasionally, she stopped to smell the canine roses visited earlier by other neighborhood pets.

They rounded the second turn, when the two Terriers who lived on the other side of the street issued Allie a direct challenge: "We dare you to come into our yard!" Allie gave a sudden tug on the lead and was suddenly free!

Barking and laughing, she bounded across the street. Dad stood in stunned silence, leash and collar in hand. Then the reality of the problem smacked him between the eyes, as he took off running after Allie. Fortunately, Allie had only sprinted across the street towards the Terriers.

Dad ran up behind Allie, and just as he reached out to catch her, she took off along the Terriers' fence line, with the Terriers running along the inside of the fence, barking their disapproval. Shortly behind came my sixty-five-year-old father, scooper in one hand and leash in the other.

Soon neighbors came outside or stood at their front door to witness the commotion. Allie ran and barked, the Terriers followed, and Dad brought up the rear. Each time when he was just about to catch Allie, she took off again.

Dad became irate. "Allie, get back here. Allie, come! Allie, stay!" Dad hurried after her.

This went on for a while. Then Allie headed up the street and down the center of the road. Dad's fear of her getting hit by a car grew greater. He picked up his pace running after her, but to no avail.

Just about the time when it seemed Dad would never catch up with Allie, a man and his dog crested the hill. Allie bolted toward them. When she reached the Basset Hound, she danced around wildly. They were obviously friends. Dad huffed up to the top of the hill, too.

"Why, you must be Allie's grandfather," the fellow with the Basset stated.

Breathing heavily, Dad said, "Well, hell, yes, I'm her grandfather. Can't you see the resemblance?"

"My name is Graves. This is our daughter Daisy. She and Allie are good buddies."

"It's nice to meet you. Thank you for corralling Allie. I was starting to become concerned that she might get hit by a car."

"Yep, I know," Mr. Graves said. "A person has got to be mighty careful when he lets his dog roam free without a collar."

Dad stood there with the collar in his hand. "Well, this particular type came loose real easily."

Mr. Graves took a look at the collar. "Yeah, these types come loose real easily if you don't know how to latch them correctly."

This reprimand irritated my father. "Oh, I didn't put it on her," Dad began, then stopped. "No matter, I've got her now."

Dad carefully slipped the collar on Allie under Mr. Graves's watchful eye. Allie finished smelling every crack and crevice, as well as Daisy, and then Dad and Allie turned around to go home. When they rounded the last corner, Allie had yet to relieve herself. Mom was at the front door when they arrived in the front yard.

"Did she do everything?" Mom asked.

"Well no, I don't think she did," my dad responded emphatically.

"Well, keep on walking."

Dad began to argue, then thought better of it and turned around to take his second lap around the block. When they rounded the last corner the second time around, they saw Mr. Graves and Daisy once again.

"Couldn't get enough the first time, eh?" Mr. Graves asked.

"Just doing some grandfatherly bonding," my dad forced a smile.

With the second trip around the block nearly completed, Allie took pity upon Dad and deposited a large stool on the neighbor's yard. While Dad bent over and picked up the excrement, he happened to glance up to see our neighbor peering out the front door. The expression on her face gave the edict, "Don't you dare leave that dog crap in my yard!" Dad didn't.

When they arrived home, Allie pranced into the house panting, eyes bright, face smiling.

Later that day we headed to the Applefest, a community activity held every October in Weston. As in many small towns, people of Weston are proud of their community.

We stopped at the first booth, where various uses for apples were displayed. Mr. Graves stood behind the counter. Lying on the ground at the back of the booth in the shade was a panting Basset Hound.

"Hello, Mr. Graves," I said. "Hello, Daisy. How are you two doing?"

"Quite well," Mr. Graves said, as Daisy's tail wagged her greeting.

"Let me introduce you to my parents," I said. "This is my mom and . . ."

"This is Allie's grandpa," Mr. Graves interrupted. "Allie already introduced us. Now that I've met your folks, I can see that Allie does favor your father." Then, turning to my dad, he continued, "We sure enjoy your son and his wife. And oh, that Allie, what a dog."

"Yes, what a dog," Dad chimed in half-heartedly.

"It's always good to have young people move in," Mr. Graves said.

"Are you a native to Weston?" Mom inquired.

"Oh, no," Mr. Graves said. "We've been here only forty-five years. Nope, we moved here from the old country."

"The old country?" Mom asked. "Is that Ireland?"

"Oh no, ma'am. Kentucky!" Mr. Graves replied.

You've got to love the people of Weston and their dogs.

CHAPTER 8

Love Handles: *More to Adore*

Allie's appetite grew with each passing year. She seemed to be in direct competition with her pal Daisy Graves. A Basset Hound should weigh about forty to fifty-five pounds, but Daisy looked to be about sixty. A Basset Hound's ears often drag along the ground. For Daisy, not only did her ears touch the ground, so did her belly. She was swaybacked, with short stocky legs and a classic Basset Hound bark, or maybe "yawp" would be a more descriptive way to put it.

Allie was now nearly five years old. One afternoon after bathing her, Tracy called me at the clinic.

"I think Allie's got a growth on her side."

"Have you noticed this before?"

"No."

"It seems to have come up rather suddenly. Better call Dr. Farris." Dr. Farris, our new vet in Weston, worked Allie in late that afternoon.

All afternoon, Tracy's mind dwelled on the many possibilities a tumor would suggest. What if this is cancer? The C word engulfed her with fear. She's too young to have cancer, isn't she? She doesn't look sick. Should we have caught this earlier? Will she have to have chemotherapy? Do dogs lose all their hair with chemo? What if she only has a few months to live?

At four forty, Tracy took Allie to the vet. "We're a little early," she apologized.

"That's fine, have a seat," the receptionist said pleasantly. "We'll be right with you."

Allie was a coward when it came to vets and animal hospitals. She sat on Tracy's lap shaking like a leaf. Normally, Tracy would try and soothe Allie, but this time she was preoccupied with her own thoughts. She tried to calm her inner fears. But she was already certain of the inevitable.

Finally, it was time to see Dr. Farris. "Come on back, Allie, and bring your mother with you." Dr. Farris was a small woman with calm mannerisms and a happy demeanor. "So what exactly are you worried about with Allie?"

"I think she has a growth, a tumor," Tracy said, placing her hand upon the prominent tissue on Allie's side.

Dr. Farris reached under Tracy's hand and felt Allie's side. She then turned Allie on the table so Allie faced her, and placed her other hand on Allie opposite the growth.

"This right here?" Dr. Farris asked.

Tracy reached alongside the vet's hand and felt the lump between her fingers. "Yes, this tumor here on Allie's right side."

"Oh, I see what you mean. Hmm, um hmm." The vet felt up and down Allie's side, belly and hindquarters. After a moment, she burst into laughter.

Tracy was shocked. How could Dr. Farris find any humor at a time like this?

"What this is," the vet began, "what this is, is a lump of fat. There's an identical one on the other side. In lay terms, we call these 'love handles.'"

At first Tracy was embarrassed, but her relief far outweighed her embarrassment, and she too began to laugh.

"So my little Allie isn't so little, after all?"

"She's actually just fat."

"Nothing else is wrong?"

"Nope, that's it. Rolls of fat! She'll be fine. You might want to watch her diet, though."

Around five thirty I called home. "Well, what's the news?" I asked cautiously when Tracy answered the phone.

"Oh, it's nothing."

"Nothing? But you were pretty certain and pretty upset that it was something."

"You shouldn't overreact or get so worried," Tracy stated. "She's just fat!"

We placed Allie on a diet. She didn't like it and in the beginning spent much time scratching on the refrigerator door. When she wanted to eat, she stood in front of the refrigerator, placed her paw on the door and then dragged her paw vertically down the door. If she got no response, she waited for about a minute and then repeated the entire process. The first scratch was gentle. But each time she scratched harder, till her nails made a loud noise across the door.

Over the next months, Allie lost a pound or two. Her love handles became love bumps. With an occasional anal-gland expression, everything regarding her health seemed to be in check. Even if she remained a little overweight, so what? She was our Allie, and we loved her just the way she was.

CHAPTER 9

More Than She Can Stomach:
Allie Gets Crohn's

Allie decided early on that she would be my own personal instructor when it came to teaching me how to relax. Apparently, she innately knew that I benefited from learning how to kick back and enjoy the simple pleasures in life, like playing with her.

Besides being a relaxation instructor Allie assumed an additional role. She taught us about parenthood. Without much fanfare or noise, Tracy and I were beginning to appreciate routines and consistencies regarding Allie's and our own schedules. Years later, when I would reflect back, it became clear that Allie had aided our growth and development as parents and had helped shape our child-rearing skills. I marveled how our canine daughter could have so many different influences on our lives.

Months had passed since our fence in Weston was completed. Allie had settled into a new routine of heading out to her own backyard in the evening rather than going on a walk around the block—a welcome reprieve for Tracy and me. One evening Tracy and I decided to treat

Allie to a stroll around the neighborhood. We put on Allie's collar and leash, grabbed the scoop and headed out the front door.

Upon rounding the first corner, I could see the Terriers in their fenced-in yard. Allie immediately jogged toward their home. When reaching their yard, Allie trotted up to their fence. She took great pleasure in strutting parallel to the fence while the Terriers were penned inside. Then she squatted and urinated in their yard—an ornery, daring action that elicited the reaction she desired—the Terriers barked and carried on hysterically. Then she peeled out, digging and kicking her back legs, grass flying. Kicking her hind legs quickly, like a dragster burning rubber, was a new behavior.

I reached down to scoop up the excrement, when a flash of red caught my eye. I stopped and reexamined the stool lying upon the scoop. Sure enough, there was a mixture of dark and bright-red blood mixed within the waste.

"You seen that before?" I asked Tracy.

"What?"

"Have you ever seen blood in her stool?"

"Where?"

"Right here in her stool."

"No. What does it mean?"

"It could mean several things." I tried to downplay the most serious.

"Like what?"

"Oh, hemorrhoids, anal fissures, trauma from constipation." I stopped short of saying the C word. Now it was my turn to fill in all the scary blanks.

We resumed our walk. Before we reached the final turn toward home, my thoughts had progressed to where Allie had cancer and would be gone before the month was out. My mind and a little medical knowledge were a recipe for disaster in the form of mental anguish.

The next morning Tracy made an appointment with Dr. Farris. Before Allie was to see the doctor that afternoon, we retrieved a fresh stool sample for lab analysis to test for blood. Only one problem: Allie was a creature of habit. Her strict routine included eating her second meal at six P.M. Then she explored the backyard for the exact spot to contribute to the nitrogen deficiency in our soil.

However, the appointment was scheduled for four. Tracy had thought this through and was several steps ahead. She fed Allie two and a half hours early, at three thirty. Although Allie was surprised, she did not argue. Upon completing her evening meal, Tracy took Allie for a stroll around the neighborhood.

Allie must have sensed she was under the gun. Tracy remained dogmatic and walked Allie all over the neighborhood until she successfully deposited her feces right into the plastic baggie Tracy forced behind Allie's tail at the precise moment when Allie took her four-point stance. The demands and expectations medical science places upon patients to gain an accurate diagnosis can be challenging. The collection took nearly thirty minutes.

Tracy and Allie arrived at the animal clinic promptly. Without any delay, they went directly into the examination room with Susan, the doctor's assistant. Even with recent material to rib Tracy about Allie's love handles, Dr. Farris remained professional.

"So you noticed some blood in Allie's stool?" She began.

"Yes, while walking her yesterday."

"How sure are you that there was blood in her stool?"

"It was definitely blood."

"Were you successful at collecting a fresh stool sample?"

Tracy produced the plastic bag filled with natural goodies. "Here it is. Doesn't that look like blood?"

Dr. Farris examined the waste in the bag. "I'd have to agree that is most likely blood. We'll hemocult test it to be certain. Susan, please test this for blood." Dr. Farris handed off Allie's specimen, then started her examination. She felt Allie's love handles and continued the physical. "I don't find anything out of the ordinary. I'd like to draw her blood and check her iron level and chemistry panel."

"How long will that take?" Tracy asked.

"We should have this back tomorrow."

"Okay. What are you looking for?"

"We need to see if she's been bleeding for any length of time. If she has, her hemoglobin and hematocrit, her iron count, would be decreased."

"Let's say it is," Tracy probed. "Then what?"

"Let's start from the other end. What if it's normal? If the hemoglobin and hematocrit are normal and the other lab studies are normal, then we should watch and wait. But if the hemoglobin and hematocrit are decreased, then we need to discuss further testing."

"Like what?" Tracy persisted.

"Ultimately, she would be best served by getting scoped."

"You mean a colonoscopy?" Tracy asked. "You do that in dogs?"

"She would have to see a G.I. specialist, a gastroenterologist." Dr. Farris explained. "There's an internist in Overland Park, Kansas."

Susan returned to the examination room with a folded hemoccult card in her hand. "It's positive," she stated.

"I expected that," the doctor said. "Let's draw her blood." She turned to Tracy, "Can you return tomorrow around one to discuss the results?"

"Can we make it three? Then Kipp can come along," Tracy requested. Every Wednesday afternoon I stopped seeing patients at one o'clock. The next couple of hours were generally consumed with administrative duties and catchup work. Tracy knew I should be available by three.

"Sure. Three P.M. it is."

In typical fashion, Allie yelped and put up a struggle while Susan restrained her and Dr. Farris drew her blood. Tracy consoled Allie until the blood had been drawn, then bade farewell until the next day.

At two fifty the next afternoon, Tracy, Allie and I headed to Dr. Farris's office for consultation. She got right down to business.

"Her labs show some concerning levels. She is slightly anemic. Her H & H are decreased. Her electrolytes are normal, but her liver enzymes and specifically her sedimentary rate are mildly elevated."

"What are you thinking?" I asked.

"Her liver has sustained some type of an insult. I hope there isn't a growth in her colon that has spread to her liver."

"What do you recommend?" I continued. "A CAT scan? Or a PET scan?"

"No," Dr. Farris said. "I think she needs a scope."

"When and where?" I pressed further.

"We've already tentatively scheduled an appointment for her with the internist on Monday morning. Can you have her down there by eight?"

I directed a questioning glance toward Tracy.

"That's pretty early," Tracy said, "but I can do it." Tracy downplayed her aversion to early-morning commitments.

"We have a prep kit that you need to use to clean out Allie's colon. You'll also place her on a strict diet starting Saturday night and continuing into Sunday. Put the tablets in her food beginning Saturday evening. Then on Monday, she must be NPO (Nothing Per Oral), nothing by mouth."

"Not that money is important here—she is our four-legged daughter—but how much are we talking for a scope?" I asked.

"I understand your concern," the vet said. "It's not cheap, but it's not too bad. The cost of the scope, including the sedation, is three hundred and twenty-five dollars. Then there's the lab expense, about seventy-five dollars. So the whole cost is about four hundred dollars. Little cheaper than having a person scoped, isn't it, Doc?" Like a well-served tennis ball, she transferred my practical concerns over the cost of animal medicine back to human medicine.

My first inclination was to aggressively return her serve, but I paused, then chose a different response. "I'd have to agree," I said mildly. Save your political thoughts about the cost of medicine for a different time and day, I silently advised myself.

Allie took her medicine in stride but protested the no-food order on Monday morning prior to her procedure. One of our neighbors, Karen, who was a dog lover and the mother of two six-month-old boys, offered to go along with Tracy for moral support. The possibility of cancer loomed on the horizon.

Karen was ready to go at six forty-five. Soon, the twins, Karen, Tracy, and Allie were positioned in the SUV and headed into the city.

The specialty animal surgical center looked state-of-the-art. Its outward appearance alone was reassuring. Tracy presented Allie for her appointment at eight as instructed. Upon handing Allie over to an aloof vet assistant, Tracy lost her composure and broke down in tears. "Take care of her," she demanded.

"We always do," the woman responded curtly. "Be back here by ten to pick her up and discuss the findings with the doctor." Then Allie was whisked from Tracy's arms, quickly disappearing behind closed doors that read, NO ADMITTANCE. STAFF ONLY!

After two anxious hours, Tracy, Karen and the kids returned to the animal hospital. Around ten fifteen, a man entered the waiting room with Allie in his hands.

"Tracy?" He asked, although Allie had already pointed out her master. She briefly perked up from her post-sedated state, wagged her tail and licked Tracy's hand as she reached out to hold her.

"Come into the examination room and let's talk."

His manner and tone sent Tracy's mind racing. It must be bad news, she surmised.

"I'll stay out here with the twins." Karen gracefully removed herself. "I'll be here if you need me."

By now Tracy had switched into autopilot. She moved in deliberate slow motion into the examination room. The fear of bad news paralyzed her thoughts and controlled her musculoskeletal system. She fixed her eyes on the internist's face, studying his expression for any clue of the diagnosis. She waited pensively for him to speak.

"The procedure went fine," he began. "I saw the entire colon. I also located the site of inflammation and probable site responsible for the bleeding. I took a couple of biopsies—pieces of tissue—and studied them under the microscope. The stain gave us a conclusive diagnosis."

Tracy could barely take it. Her thoughts raced, and the voice in her head was screaming, "All right, already. What is it? What does Allie have?" Yet outwardly she remained calm and collected.

"What I have concluded . . ." the vet continued to drag out his answer, like a skilled politician evading a difficult question, ". . . is that Allie has Crohn's disease."

"Crohn's disease?" Tracy repeated his words out loud.

"Yes. It's an inflammatory disease of the intestines. In most cases, we can control it with diet, but occasional flare-ups will need medication to effectively treat the acute events."

His demeanor remained distant and clinical. "I would recommend you try some specific brands and flavors of dog food until you find the one that best suits your pet," he said. "Lamb and rice or turkey and rice are two of the most effective. Here's some literature with practical suggestions that will help her, but mostly this is about diet."

"It's not cancer?" Tracy's thoughts, like a broken movie reel playing over and over in her mind, remained stuck on the gripping fears of cancer.

"No, it's not cancer."

Out of sheer relief, Tracy asked the question one more time. "So you are saying Allie does not have cancer?"

"That's right. It's Crohn's disease," he patiently repeated. "I think she'll do just fine if you can control her diet," he said, ushering Tracy and Allie out of the consultation room. "Our staff will check you out."

Tracy was overjoyed. Allie seemed jubilant as well, even in her post-anesthetized state.

On the ride back, Tracy and Karen concluded that although the facility looked good, the staff and the doctor were missing those extra qualities that make these difficult, and expensive, experiences palatable-bedside manner and compassion.

Tracy dropped Karen and the twins off at home and drove straight to the clinic. I had been seeing patients that morning but must admit I had been distracted with my thoughts of Allie and the fears of what might lie ahead.

My nurse, Marsha, interrupted me from a patient room. "Doctor, you have a quick, but urgent call," she said.

I excused myself briefly, then headed toward my office. There sat Allie and Tracy in my desk chair.

"So?" I asked, straining to interpret Tracy's expression.

"It's not great, but it could be much worse."

"What is it?"

"Crohn's disease."

"Crohn's disease?"

"Yep, Crohn's."

"Well, butter my buns, and call me biscuit. She's just like a person. Her symptoms are just like a human's. That never crossed my mind," I admitted.

Tracy gave me the literature, then briefly retold their experience.

"Crohn's," I said once again. "Boy, Allie doesn't know how bad this is. The way she likes to eat, this could cramp her style—better than cramping her gut, I s'pose." I smiled at my own wit.

"You know, this is amazing. I should have figured out this diagnosis on my own," I continued. "Besides Allie having the classic symptoms of blood in her stool, I should at least have thought of the possibility of Crohn's."

"Why is that?" Tracy finally took the bait I'd been dangling in front of her.

"Well, Crohn's is familial. It has a genetic tendency. I've told my family that since I have an uncle with Crohn's, one day one of us would show up with it, probably one of our children, as it often skips a generation.

Who would have guessed the next time Crohn's showed up in our family it would be in our four-legged daughter, Allie!"

CHAPTER 10

Princess Allie: *The Inside Bichon Story*

One afternoon when Tracy and I were in Kansas City for the day, we met a young man who was in vet school. Our conversation led to discussions of dogs, which ultimately led to a discussion of Bichon Frises and, of course, Allie.

"I have an interesting story about a Bichon," he told us. "A wealthy woman drove up in her Jaguar to the vet clinic where I was working as an intern. Through the front window of the clinic, I observed her exiting her car, carrying a cute little bundle of white fur. Once in the office she said, 'I'm here to see the doctor.' 'Your name?' I asked. 'I'm Mrs. Wellington, and this is my dog.' A lady sitting next to the window said, 'Oh, what a cute little dog. Is that a Poodle?' With utmost disdain, the lady responded, 'This is a Bitchin Frizze!'"

Prior to Allie, I knew nothing about Bichon Frises. I found this strange, having grown up in a household with a veterinarian and with pets all my life. When I had asked Mom to locate the right breed for Tracy, little did I know how wise and insightful her decision would be.

The Bichon was bred to be a companion dog.

Like the Poodle and many other curly-coated dogs that originated in Europe, the Bichon is a descendent of the Barbet or Water Spaniel. In fact, the earliest Water Spaniel type Bichons were used as hunting dogs, to retrieve fowl from waters. But the breed proved to be smaller than the Water Spaniel and quickly developed into a true companion dog, discarding the official role of hunter.

Bichons were the perfect breed for one noble dog lover. In the late sixteenth century, King Henry III, a French monarch, owned several Bichons. He loved his canine companions so much that he did not wish to be separated from them for any length of time during the day. He, therefore, developed a wicker basket that was hung around his neck with ribbons. Seated in the man-made carrier was his pet Bichon. The king was said to stroll around the imperial courts and conduct his royal affairs with his favorite pet always at his fingertips.

The ladies of the royal court followed the king's lead, adorning themselves with small dogs, generally Bichons, clutched under their arm or wrapped in the folds of their gown or shawl. These little dogs were treated as if they had descended from noble lineage. On some basic level, I could relate to this. Sometimes Allie had an air of superiority and unmitigated self-confidence. I now understood this was a characteristic of her breed.

Allie's self-confidence carried over into her natural instincts as a hunter. She reverted to acting like a dog on the hunt. Durable and sturdy, she had blazing fast speed. In tip-top shape, she weighed about thirteen pounds. She often stood in our backyard with one paw held up and her curved tail pointing straight back while focusing on some small, unsuspecting prey. She derived great pleasure from tormenting innocent bunnies and squirrels as she attempted to sneak up behind them.

Allie also attacked hard-boiled Easter eggs with a vengeance. Tracy and I spent hours playing the "egg game" with her. One of us would cock our arm in a throwing motion and then fake throwing hard-boiled eggs off the deck into the far corners of our yard. Allie would prance like a reindeer across the grass and in midstride realize we hadn't thrown the egg yet. She would look up at us intently, pointing like a Retriever, begging us to quit faking and throw. I often thought she could have given Cool Hand Luke a run for his money in the race to eat fifty hard-boiled eggs in one hour.

We met one Bichon that could have out-eaten Allie. His name was Casper, and he belonged to one of Tracy's coworkers at school. The first time we met Casper, Tracy and I were flabbergasted. He was the size of a standard Poodle, nearly six times larger than Allie, and weighed about eighty pounds. Allie and Casper hit it off and spent many afternoons together when we dropped her off for a play date with her BCFF (best canine friend forever.)

There were two Bichons of some notoriety in the last decade in America. One was the Bichon J. R., who was grand-champion dog at the Westminster national dog show. When I saw that a Bichon was the champion, for a moment I wondered what might have been if Allie had taken to obedience school.

The second Bichon of notoriety was a very unfortunate dog. In the summer of 2001, traffic had gotten extremely congested on one of the busiest freeways in California. One man lost his temper. He got out of his car, reached through an open car window, and in a flash snatched a Bichon Frise named Leo, who was seated on his master's lap. With the force of a world class-hammer thrower, he flung the innocent little creature into oncoming traffic and to his untimely death. I'll never forget this horrific incident, as this little dog had been just like Allie.

Upon hearing the story, Tracy and I vowed to be careful while driving with Allie on our lap, especially with her head out the window. We counted our blessings daily for our strong-willed, independent, lovable little Bitchin Frizze, Chelsea Alexis.

Chapter 11

From Princess to Drama Queen:
Allie's Instant Recovery

One evening we went to bed with Allie, as usual, sprawled out between us. Her skin was soft and smooth. The next morning Allie's skin had suddenly developed the texture of a hedgehog. Her immune system and her integumentary system, the largest system in the body known as the skin, had suddenly gone haywire.

There lay Allie on her back, her four legs pointing toward the ceiling. Her paws were relaxed, and each leg was bent at the joint. I reached over to pat her belly. She stirred.

I stroked her back and felt a bump between my fingers, then a second, then a third . . . The mental fog reserved for the early morning suddenly lifted. In an instant, all my neurons fired in order and in unison. "What's all over Allie?" I was now fully awake.

I examined her skin. The growths were too numerous to count. Upon close and thorough examination, I noticed that these small lesions were often mildly red and inflamed, and in the center of most of them was a prominent pore. They looked liked infected pimples, but the growths were more complex than pimples and represented an inflamed sweat gland—a whole host of sweat glands.

Several months had passed uneventfully since we had found blood in Allie's stool and she had been diagnosed with Crohn's, and we had been lulled into a false sense of security that all was right with her health. But now a few cysts had multiplied in size and number almost overnight. Throughout Allie's life, we had observed a small pimple-like nodule here and an inflamed bump there. When a lesion or two popped up, we figured this was not unlike a breakout of acne during adolescence. But that all changed immediately.

Allie didn't seem bothered by it. She hadn't even become irritated or put upon with my sudden interest in probing and examining her entire body. I suspected she had mistaken my vigorous palpation for a well-deserved massage.

By eight A.M., we contacted the Weston vet clinic, and Allie was scheduled for an eleven o'clock office visit. When asked the reason for the visit, I replied, "Acute wart eruption."

Dr. Farris was nearly as surprised as we were. Because of Allie's thick and stylish fur, at first glance her appearance was normal. But upon closer observation, she clearly had become afflicted with some rare disease.

"These look like sebaceous cysts!" Dr. Farris exclaimed.

"But there are so many, and they arose so instantaneously," I answered.

"She doesn't seem to be in any pain. I'd like to consult a Bichon dermatology specialist. I'll call you with my recommendations and treatment after I consult with my colleague."

Later that day, Dr. Farris called. "This is an interesting medical condition specific to this breed," she reported. "In Bichons there is an increased chance of developing sebaceous cysts. Generally, it's not sudden or as extreme. But it can be, and with Allie, it obviously is."

"What do we do for her?"

"The specialist said sometimes a burst of steroids helps. And let's also give a five-day course of antibiotics. If we don't see any improvement, we may have to remove the cysts surgically."

"That's just what we don't need," I thought out loud, pondering silently what type of post-surgical patient Allie would be. I hated the thought of Allie having to undergo surgery. She hadn't proved the most stoic of patients on her few past medical encounters. But, I rationalized, if she had to undergo surgery, this probably wouldn't be a bad one. There would be no incision deeper than her skin. Whenever the abdominal cavity remained intact, the surgery has a greater chance of success. Yet, knowing she faced this tugged heavily on my heart. Perhaps she'll respond to the medication, I hoped.

Once again Allie provided me a good example. She had taken the Crohn's diet in stride and adapted to change with minimum trouble. She liked the lamb and rice and the lamb Pupperoni treats. I suspected it was more about quantity than quality with Allie's palate. If I could learn to take personal struggles and life challenges in stride like Allie, I'd probably find more pleasure in life. I'll have to work on that, I told myself.

Allie's latest condition reminded me of a very unusual skin condition in humans that occurs as a sudden and severe allergic type of reaction to particular medications, like some antibiotics. This is known as Steven's Johnson Syndrome. In this rare condition, the patient's skin literally sloughs off. This event is so sudden that it is often misdiagnosed in the first twenty-four to forty-eight hours due to the unique nature and instant insult throughout the body.

A second medical malady, known as neurofibromatosis—also known as Vonrecklinghouse Syndrome—occurs gradually. (Much debate continues regarding the actual diagnosis of the Elephant Man. Neurofibromatosis ranks near the top of the list.) Small neurofibromas, nerve sheath tumors, develop along nerves throughout various locations within the body. Nerves, the millions of "electrical wires" that run all over our body, tell the muscles to move when the brain commands an action, that something is touching our skin. Basically, anywhere the patient has a nerve (which is anywhere and everywhere), a small clump of tissue may grow. Tender soft-tissue growths develop under the skin.

These people are distinctively different looking. They have multiple growths all over their skin.

Many neurofibromas are in locations that allow effective covering with loose-fitting clothing. A less fortunate group develop wartlike, neurofibromas on the visible skin, like the face, neck, arms, and hands. Disfigurement is often the end result. As in the case of the Elephant Man, the degree of severity can be deforming and debilitative.

For Allie, she had warts of various sizes and shapes, all over her skin, including such unusual locations as on her nose, her paws, and her tail. These fluid-filled, encapsulated cysts, over night, were everywhere. She was beginning to resemble the Elephant Man.

Weeks passed. A season had come and gone. The medication had not slowed the progression of her condition. If anything, the steroids had only stimulated Allie's already vigorous appetite. The cysts became more prevalent and inflamed in the summer.

Since, several of the swollen glands were causing Allie some discomfort, we decided she must undergo surgery. Dr. Farris agreed.

We coordinated our calendars and chose to have the operation on a Friday so I would be available over the weekend for assistance. I was more than willing to take time off on the day of Allie's surgery.

Friday morning we took Allie to the animal hospital. Dr. Farris and her staff told us we should return around four o'clock that afternoon.

When we returned, we were surprised at Allie's post-surgical appearance—she had gauze wrapped around her belly. Dr. Farris had shaved patches of fur from more than fifteen locations throughout her body. Allie moved gingerly and was still somewhat sedated.

"I took off twenty-three cysts!" Dr. Farris stated proudly. "Five of them were deep, and those required the most extensive sutures. I've identified them with black suture. The smaller ones have the purple suture."

Allie whimpered when we picked her up. I felt sorry for her. She was distraught and uncomfortable. With surgical sites and sores all over her body, we had no way to pick her up without touching several tender areas. She looked like she had been in a serious dogfight and lucky to survive.

The weekend presented challenges. At first Allie couldn't lie down. Whichever position she tried, she bumped several of the surgical sites, causing pain. Her only comfortable position was standing, head and tail down, partly leaning against the side of her cage. For the first twenty-four hours, she looked pathetic, puny and extremely vulnerable.

By Monday she was tiptoeing around without assistance, but she could not jump up on her chair or climb stairs. We weaned her off her pain meds. She continued to whimper and whine when we picked her up or placed her in her cage.

After taking the weekend off from our home project, our carpenter, Benny, resumed his work on Monday. Since we had moved to Weston, Benny spent most of the daylight hours at our house, remodeling our money-pit, fixer-upper. It had become a full-time job.

Benny had grown fond of Allie over the months. He couldn't help laughing when he first laid eyes on her. The tufts of hair between the numerous bald spots covering Allie's body were a sight. Even though convalescing, she detected Benny's amusement. For the first time since the surgery, she must have realized how silly she looked. Her expression and reaction suggested she was embarrassed—she hid her eyes in shame. Her response to Benny instantly transformed his response from outward enjoyment to compassion and empathy.

After several days, Allie's wounds began to heal, but she was still uncomfortable. She tried desperately to scratch, but her claws kept getting caught in her sutures. Several of the wounds were pulled open with her incessant scratching—a behavior that forced our hand. We placed Allie in an Elizabethan collar for the second time in her life, a decision she protested. She hadn't changed all that much over the years; she had protested just as vehemently the first time we placed this type of collar around her neck when we had her spayed as a young dog. She made both of us feel guilty and sorry for her, back then and now.

Since the surgery, Tracy had remained at Allie's side, responding to her every need. On the seventh day after surgery, Tracy had a previous commitment and decided it was the right time to give Allie some space.

"Benny, will you keep an eye on Allie for me?" she asked our carpenter. "I'll be back in about two hours."

"Sure," Benny agreed.

Tracy hugged Allie and bade her farewell. Then she gently put Allie in her cage and placed a handful of Pupperoni treats in with her. Allie sulked and whimpered, declining the succulent treats she usually savored. Tracy felt sorry for her as she gave Benny final instructions before leaving.

When she returned, Benny was all smiles. "What's so funny?" Tracy asked.

"It's Allie," Benny said.

"What about her?"

"No sooner had the garage door closed than her entire demeanor changed. She didn't know I was watching her. She hopped up, ate the treats, lapped up some water, stretched and then sprawled out on her side."

"Seriously?"

"She's quite the little actor." Benny said. "Close to an Oscar performance, real convincing."

Tracy stood there perplexed. "And all this time, I thought she was legit. I wonder how long she's been playing me."

"How long have you had her?"

"Around five years," Tracy replied.

Benny smiled. "I'd say about five years!"

CHAPTER 12

Allie Visits St. Louis: *The Not-So-Perfect Houseguest*

Time heals all wounds. Allie recovered from her cyst surgery in about a month. Her fur grew and covered the many surgical sites on her skin. But she always had at least a handful of cysts. We tried every orthodox and most unorthodox treatment options we could find, but we never could get control of her overproductive endocrine system. Even though she had at least five more surgeries throughout her life, she never got used to the recovery process.

We observed her overall health stabilize throughout the next several years. Provided we kept her on a strict diet, her Crohn's remained controlled. But the mere suggestion of feeding her beef or table scraps sent her gut was into a tailspin.

The remodeling project took shape, and our fixer-upper was becoming a home. But the daily disruption of our house and our lives was getting on our nerves. Our renovation had been going on for about one year. We needed an escape, and Tracy's college reunion was the perfect respite.

We decided to call upon Tracy's kin for dog-sitter duties. Allie would not stay in a kennel. Tracy would not allow it. So Tracy's parents agreed to watch her for us. However, they would most effectively handle Allie on their own turf.

"No home-court advantage," I told Allie the morning before we left for Tracy's Florida College reunion by way of St. Louis. From Weston to St. Louis was a four-and-a-half hour jaunt. We would drive across the state that morning, deliver Allie at Tracy's parents' home, then fly to Tampa, arriving in mid-afternoon.

We arrived in St. Louis shortly after noon; our flight was to depart at three thirty for the Sunshine State. We unloaded Allie's luggage. Like many women, she traveled with much paraphernalia: her cage, a tub of food, an Ace-wrapped chew toy, and an unlimited supply of Pupperonis.

Allie had spent significant time at the Gavin household when she was a puppy and while we lived in St. Louis. Tracy's parents, John and Alice, were German Shepherd lovers and currently had a four-legged daughter, Pippin One. She was an energetic, eighty-pound, one-year-old, high-strung puppy. She also thought she was a lapdog. Except for the furniture, Pippin had the run of the house.

John was a strict, no-nonsense man. He believed a dog's place was on the floor. Pippin respected him and complied with his rules, like everyone else in his family. A calm, smooth-sailing atmosphere was the standard of the Gavin household.

Even though John and Alice were experienced grandparents, as parents of a precious pooch, we felt compelled to remind them of their responsibilities.

We outlined a strict schedule:

7:00 A.M. Feed Allie breakfast.

7:15 A.M. After breakfast take Allie outside.

10:00 A.M. Feed Allie Pupperoni.

10:05 A.M. Play with Allie if you have time.

10:30 A.M. Nap time—Let her sleep until 11:00.

11:00 A.M. Feed Allie Pupperoni.

12:00 Noon Take Allie outside.

12:10 P.M. Play with Allie if time permits.

1:30 P.M. Nap time—Let her sleep until 2:00.

2:00 P.M. Take Allie outside.

6:00 P.M. Feed Allie supper.

6:10 P.M. Feed Allie one half a Pupperoni.

6:15 P.M. Walk Allie around the neighborhood.

9:00 P.M. Feed Allie Pupperoni.

9:10 P.M. Take Allie outside.

10:00 P.M. Put Allie to bed.

"Certainly, Tracy," John responded after Tracy briefed him on his and Alice's assignments. "We don't have anything else to do but care for your little dog, except I have a full-time job, and your mother has a household to run."

Alice drove us to the airport. "Take care of Allie and pamper your granddaughter!" Tracy instructed her mother upon our departure.

"She'll be fine," her mother reassured us.

In all our planning for Allie, we had neglected to factor in Pippin. Pippin thought Allie was a plaything, one of those fluffy toys that she could pick up with her teeth, place between her jaws and then squeeze. Allie wanted nothing to do with this.

Pippin wore an electric collar and had an electric boundary both inside and out. The outside electric fence surrounded the yard. Pippin was smart and had learned how to maneuver around the property without triggering a jolt of current. Inside, the electric boundary prevented Pippin from going into the bedrooms and the family room, where the sofa and sitting chairs were located.

Allie, on the other hand, had free run of the house. Pippin chased her around, trying to catch her and squeeze her between her teeth. Allie, not wanting anything to do with Pippin, realized almost immediately what rooms Pippin was forbidden to enter. Once she had figured this out, she tormented Pippin. Allie raced nimbly from the bedroom to the kitchen and lay down under the kitchen table. Pippin bounded after. Allie scampered into the family room. Pippin wanted desperately to follow, but the sting of electric current was greater than her natural desire.

Pippin would whine and carry on. Within moments, she triggered a reaction from John:

"Pippin! Knock it off!"

Then she would slink away with her tail between her legs.

Seeing Pippin slink away only got Allie going again. Allie darted across the floor to the safety of her bedroom. Pippin saw Allie fly across the room and chased after her. Allie managed to pull off this stealth tactic several times per day, each time eliciting the same reaction from John: "Pippin, knock it off!"

John did not appreciate Allie hopping up on the couch. So when she did, he would set her down on the floor. Allie would then walk to the other side of the couch and jump up, whereupon John would set her down again. After a couple of attempts, she changed tactics—she strolled to a chair, hopped up and lay down. Again, John would promptly set her down on the floor. But Allie was persistent and would not take no for an answer. This battle of wills went on for hours. Allie was tenacious.

The first night at the Gavins' home, Allie leaped up on John and Alice's bed to go to sleep. After all, she had been sleeping in our bed for six years. John picked her up and placed her in her cage in the other room, then shut the cage door. For fifteen minutes, Allie whimpered, whined and cried, just as she had done the first night at our house as a puppy. Surprisingly, the trick she had used as a puppy worked once again. Within twenty minutes, John went to her cage, lifted her out and placed her on the bed.

By the time Allie had been a guest in the Gavin home for five days, John was helping her jump onto the sofa, lifting her onto the bed at bedtime and even feeding her Pupperonis while she lounged next to him on his furniture. She reveled in John's attention. Like mine, John's bark was worse than his bite. Allie seemed to understand this. In fact, I believe she was teaching me and now John another important life lesson: You can teach an old dog a new trick.

When we returned to John and Alice's home, Allie was pleased but distant. I had heard people say that their pets got mad with them when they left them, but I had never believed it until that particular day. Allie ignored us and gave us the silent treatment, while showering John and Alice with uncharacteristic attention.

This lasted for about twenty-four hours. She snapped out of her attitude when we packed up the car to go back to Weston: When I picked up her cage, tub, and bag to carry them to the car, Allie sprang to her feet and trotted by my side. After waving good-bye and pulling away, Allie turned and licked Tracy on the cheek. Then she curled up on her lap and let out a heavy sigh. At that moment, all was right in her world.

CHAPTER 13

Coping With Loss: *A Ball of Living Comfort*

"Let's have a baby," Tracy said one afternoon.

"Now?"

"Not this very moment. But I'd like to start thinking about it." Tracy quickly put my hormonal instincts in their place.

Allie seemed to understand what was going on. She appeared attentive and interested in the conversation whenever we discussed having a baby. When we set out to make a baby, she stood on the bed whining and talking, as if to encourage us. She had always been interested any time we were intimate, but now her interest was far greater. Perhaps her maternal instinct had been piqued?

After many unsuccessful attempts at conception, we resorted to scientific methods, like basal body temperature charts. When this failed, we plunged deeper into the standard fertility exercises, then we resorted to the ovulation kit. This little self-administered lab test measured Tracy's hormonal changes and could predict with ninety-eight percent accuracy to the very hour when she was ovulating. If we timed it right, within twenty-four hours of this calculated monthly event, our odds of conception went up significantly.

Needless to say, the entire process was rather enjoyable. Several times when Tracy called and invited me home in the middle of the day for a rendezvous, not only did Tracy greet me at the door, so did Allie. She was equally interested and engaged in the whole baby-making process. It got a little weird.

One day, Tracy called me at work, her voice brimming with excitement. "Congratulations, Papa," she said.

Allie soon sensed the physical changes in Tracy. She provided moral support during those first few weeks of hormonal changes and mood swings associated with early pregnancy. When Tracy became moody, Allie stayed by her side. When Tracy raised her voice, Allie stared at her intently. When Tracy cried, Allie licked her hand.

During those first few weeks, Allie appeared to be going through similar changes herself. She was less playful and more cautious. I noticed she was sleeping more than usual, and seemed to move around gingerly. She lost her appetite, an extremely unusual occurrence. I speculated she might be experiencing her own sympathetic pregnancy.

Around the thirteenth week, Tracy noticed an occasional twinge of pain and some cramping, but chalked them up to the normal signs of pregnancy. When the cramping grew stronger and more frequent, she grew alarmed. Allie seemed to sense that something was wrong. She followed Tracy around the house and clung to Tracy's side. She would sit next to Tracy and lick her hand whenever Tracy experienced any pains. I, too, was concerned.

Before we could even make arrangements to meet with our doctor, Tracy's symptoms progressed to active bleeding. We made an emergency doctor's visit. After completing lab tests and a sonogram, the outcome was confirmed.

"The baby is no longer alive. Your body knows this and is trying to abort this child. We'll need to perform a D and C (dilatation and curettage)—clean out the fetal tissue from your uterus," the obstetrician told us.

Even having observed and processed all the events leading up to this doctor visit, the words made the fears and thoughts racing in our head reality. Our baby was no longer alive. We were no longer going to be parents. This was a crushing blow. In an instant, all hope was gone.

This was a difficult time. Intellectually, we could rationalize that something must have been wrong with this baby. Therefore, God had done us a huge favor. But there was a problem—it didn't feel like a huge favor. The emptiness and loneliness were palpable.

After the D and C, I brought Tracy home under strict instructions that she take it easy for the next forty-eight hours. Allie lay next to Tracy on the bed. Maybe she understood better than we realized that Tracy's pregnancy had ended in pain and loss. No little baby came home with us from the hospital.

A couple of days after the miscarriage, it dawned on me that Allie had sensed the change. She too had suffered a loss. Her false pregnancy came to an abrupt end. It hit her hard. She seemed forlorn and distraught. The energy she had always displayed now appeared to be drained from her little body. She moped around the house. When I called her for her meals, she didn't respond immediately, an extremely unusual response, given her usual ravenous appetite.

She seemed to understand that Tracy was no longer pregnant. Allie's own motherly instincts had been piqued and just as quickly dashed again. Who knows? Perhaps she had looked forward to having a baby around the house. Her actions and behavior suggested to me that she too was grieving the loss. She seemed distant and unengaged. She moped around the house. I had to force her to go on walks and encourage her to eat.

To see Allie like this bothered me. She had always seemed unflappable. Not this time. With this loss, she was devastated, just like us. For the next several weeks, Allie was right by Tracy's side. She could sense Tracy's distress, and she wanted to provide support and comfort. Not much could ease Tracy's pain, nor mine, but this gesture from Allie helped.

I had been raised with the belief that men are stoic. Seeing Allie behave like this gave me another life example. It is okay to cry. It is healthy to allow oneself to grieve. When a person or a family suffers a loss of this magnitude, it's normal to be sad. In fact, sadness is one of the stages of grief. To not experience sadness would hinder the healing process. Allie's behavior aided Tracy and me in dealing with the loss of this baby and we slowly began to heal. It took some time, but after several weeks, the brightness of the sun returned, the brilliance of colors returned, and we began to experience joy once again. Hope returned to our lives, thanks in part to Allie's attitude.

CHAPTER 14

Winning Over Granddad: *Allie's Birthday*

While I was growing up, my dad always maintained a distance from our pets. He considered few of our pets his. When Babee Snookums replaced each of us kids, it became clear Dad had changed his stance regarding pets.

The first time Dad and Mom brought their new Poodle with them on their travels, I couldn't resist saying, "I never thought I'd see the day when you'd let a damn dog rule your life. You know, Dad, dogs are better off in kennels when you and Mom travel!"

Dad had said this phrase many times over the years, and on this rare occasion he took my ribbing in stride.

One particular weekend we were meeting Mom and Dad in Manhattan, Kansas, to attend a K-State football game. They had left their dog in Salina with my sister Kim and her husband, Lynn. Once again, Tracy and I breached family etiquette and included Allie in our travels. It just so happened this weekend was her birthday.

We planned a birthday party at the hotel where we were staying for the weekend. I told Mom ahead of time, but purposefully kept Dad in the dark. Mom brought a gift for her grandpuppy, and Tracy and I bought a cake and a gift. Allie sensed this was her special day and was even more engaging than usual. She snooped in our bags. She sniffed the air as if to say, whose cake? She followed us around the room. All in all, she reminded me of an anxious child on her birthday.

After the football game, we met in the hotel lobby. I said to my parents, "You'll need to come to our room. We'll see you in ten minutes."

"What for?" Dad asked.

"For Allie's birthday party."

"Well, for crying out loud, she's just a damn dog!"

"That's fine, you can miss it, but you won't get any cake."

Dad and Allie had one characteristic in common. Neither of them had ever met a food they didn't like, and cake was no exception.

Mom and Dad arrived promptly ten minutes later.

"Where's my grandpuppy?" Mom asked and immediately picked up Allie.

Allie licked her face, then glanced at Dad and tossed her head as if to say, "Oh. You're here, too."

Mom, Tracy, and I sang *Happy Birthday* while Dad remained silent. I had a mind to say, "If you don't sing to her, you can't have any cake," but I decided against antagonizing him further—at least he had joined us.

Allie reveled in the excitement and attention. We helped her open the two presents, a chewy bone and a squeeze toy. We gushed over her, partly to show her our true feelings, partly to irritate Dad.

When her party was over and we had had our fill of cake, I forced Allie into Dad's hands. "Tell your grandpa thank you for your gift, Allie."

Dad smirked. For the first time, I sensed he kind of liked Allie. As he left the room, he said graciously, "Thanks for the cake." Only he couldn't stop there. "You know a dog's place is at home in a kennel."

I followed him down the hall and said, "You better be nice to Allie, Dad, or next year she won't invite you to her birthday party."

CHAPTER 15

Tracy's Folly: *A White Elephant Turns Gray*

Within weeks of our move to Weston, Tracy had become a distinguished member of the Swamp club—an organization named after a creek outside of Weston, Swamp Creek. Apparently, people from anywhere near this creek, when asked, would say they were from Swamp Creek. This was a women's home-extension organization, a dying breed throughout most of the country at the time we lived in Weston. The Swamp club was formed in the 1940s as a way for women to learn skills about thrift and frugality while dealing with the many demands placed upon the home in rural America. Over time, the Swamp club had become a women's social club and a way for newcomers to meet the female pillars of the community and their families.

So, when the realtor asked Tracy if she would like to join the club, she cautiously accepted the invitation.

After attending her first Swamp club meeting, Tracy came home and reported, "I'm three decades younger than the youngest member.

And what's so amazing about that is my presence lowered the average age by only two years. One lovely lady is eighty-eight."

"What did you do at the meeting?" I asked.

"Oh, we talked, ate cookies and drank punch, and planned our next activity."

"And what's that?"

"We're going to meet again, have cookies and punch, and plan our next activity. No, seriously, we're having a white elephant exchange for the holidays."

Tracy joining the Swamp club proved wise, as many of the ladies became my patients. For some reason, many people are enamored with knowing the doctor and the doctor's wife on a social level, especially, in a small town.

Our time in Weston was both personally and professionally satisfying. I delivered nearly two hundred babies in less than three years. But no matter how long we lived there, we would never be known as natives. Still, we developed many good friendships.

Against this backdrop of hospitality and kindness, and acknowledging the many ways in which we had become members of the community, we made a difficult decision—to change my career path. This time I would be returning to an area of medicine I had left only six years before.

During my relatively short stint in family practice, I had gained invaluable clinical experience, something I would always have to draw upon. However, throughout the last year I had grown bored, no longer challenged by the routine cases or the repetitive blood pressure checks and ear/nose/throat exams. I needed a challenge. What better mental stimulation than to return to academia, I figured.

So nearly three years into my family practice and our life in Weston, I announced to Tracy I thought I should return to radiology and complete the residency I had initially started back in Saint Louis, the year after Tracy and I were married. Though this decision was bittersweet, she agreed. Allie maintained her unflappable attitude and took the change in stride.

That autumn of 1996, while we planned our move, the holidays came along. Preparing our move took much of our spare time, but we determined to keep the holiday festivities and traditions intact.

Allie enjoyed the excitement of Halloween. It brought her great pleasure every time the doorbell rang and some goblin stood on the stoop, bag open, begging for candy. The second the sound of the bell pierced the air, Allie dashed to the door, spun wildly around in circles and barked excitedly. Once we opened the door, even a crack, Allie attempted to dart through and jump upon the children at the door, showing them a trick or two of her own. She also tried to steal candy whenever anyone wasn't looking and sometimes even when they were. Her sweet tooth was longer than any of her canine teeth.

Just when she had forgotten about all of the fun of Halloween, the aroma of baked turkey wafted through the air. She loved turkey and, therefore, loved Thanksgiving. She seemed in tune with the excitement central to a special day dedicated to turkey. First, she stayed near the kitchen all morning, and then she was at the door to greet the family and friends.

Thanksgiving was her favorite holiday. We consistently gave her extra helpings of turkey, which remained one of the few foods acceptable for her delicate stomach.

From Thanksgiving until Christmas, Allie sensed the excitement in the air. When I dug out the Christmas ornaments, her interest level and curiosity were instantly aroused. Over the years, she had developed a little dance that she performed whenever she was especially happy and excited. She would spin around in circles as if chasing her tail, then she'd lay her two front paws and her head on the ground with her bottom sticking straight up in the air. If we acknowledged her, she would wag her bottom, and her tail would follow. We named this ritual her "happy dance."

Since we included Allie in all our family traditions, she had her own embroidered Allie stocking. I always got a charge out of Allie when I hung up the Christmas stockings as she performed her "happy dance."

She could smell all of the treats and presents that had ever touched the stocking from Christmases past.

One of my favorite games was to put a Pupperoni or some other doggie treat in the toe of her stocking and place the sock on the floor. Allie instantly set about trying to crawl into the stocking, shoving her snout all the way down to the toe to retrieve the tasty morsel. Sometimes I placed the stocking back onto the hook along the mantelpiece. Allie sniffed, stretched and pawed as she stood under her stocking near the hearth. She would carry on for hours. Without giving in, she would dial her efforts down to simply lying on the rug in front of the fireplace, as if she were a guard dog for Fort Knox.

Every few days I added some treat or gift to her Christmas sock. When I headed toward the mantel, she knew that I was placing some new treasure into her stocking, and she happily danced her approval at my feet. Occasionally, I would break down and give her a treat from the stocking, but mostly, I made her wait until December 25, like everyone else.

We also put gifts under the tree for her. We even gave gifts to each other from Allie. I signed all correspondence and all gift cards with a paw print.

Christmas was my favorite holiday. It was already the second week of December. It would be Christmas before long.

"Don't forget, I have Swamp club tonight," Tracy reminded me one day.

"That's fine," I reassured her. "I'll bring some charts home from the clinic and complete my paperwork here at home. Allie and I will enjoy an evening at home, just the two of us."

The house was decorated in Christmas finery, which filled the home with warmth and excitement.

"We'll stare at the presents and ornaments all night." I said, and picked Allie up and squeezed her. She licked my nose, then squirmed, telling me, "Okay, I let you squeeze me. Now put me down!"

"What did you get for your white-elephant gift?" I asked, noticing a gaily wrapped box with a big red bow.

"It's a surprise." Tracy acted coy, but I could see she was pleased with her gift selection.

"Fine. But I want to hear about it when you get home."

"I'll tell you all about it, later. Bye," she said and left.

I fed Allie. Then she and I headed up to the clinic for her evening stroll around the grounds, a treat I still liked to afford her, even though she had her own fenced-in backyard. After she had relieved herself, I picked up some charts from the office, and we returned home where we sat in the front room and listened to Christmas carols. The crackle and warmth of the fire filled the room. Our tree was especially pretty that year—a tall, blue spruce, full and healthy.

I completed my charting and enjoyed the peaceful evening. About eight thirty, I heard the garage door open, and soon Tracy entered the room. Allie lay relaxed on her back with all four legs directed toward the ceiling. When Tracy came in, Allie cocked her head, sniffed the air, then turned her face toward Tracy.

Tracy reached over and scratched Allie's exposed belly. She appeared distraught. After a few seconds, she spoke, cautiously and deliberately. "That celebration was interesting."

"So what present did you get?"

Tracy left the room for a moment, then returned with a lovely silver platter.

"What's that?"

"It's the gift I received."

"Oh." I hesitated. "I thought 'white elephant' meant a gag gift."

"So did I. But it also means something that's been lying around the house that you don't use or want. I believe that's why it's called a white elephant?"

That makes no sense, I thought to myself. "So what happened?"

"After cookies and coffee, Mrs. Wilson said, 'It's time. Everyone, place your wrapped gifts in the middle of the room, and we'll draw numbers. That will decide the order of our gift selection.' Many of these ladies were giddy with excitement. I drew number seven. The first gift was a beautiful hand-knitted blanket. The next was a silver teapot. The next was a set of coasters. As the swap progressed, I knew I'd really goofed up."

"Why, what was your gift?"

"I'm getting to that!"

"What did you do?" I was intrigued with this story and anxiously awaited the outcome.

"Well, Melba Carter had number six. She picked up my gift. All eyes were on her as she opened the box carefully. She methodically and deliberately stripped the paper from the box, folded it in a neat square, and then placed it beside her on the chair. She then opened the box, reached in and pulled out a whoopee cushion."

"A whoopee cushion?" I asked incredulously.

"That's what I said, a whoopee cushion?"

"You didn't?"

"Yes, I did!"

"So, what happened?"

"Melba stared at it and then asked, 'What is it?'"

"Nobody knew what a whoopee cushion was?" I asked, trying not to laugh. "What did you do?"

"I wanted to crawl in a hole. Then I realized I was next to choose, so I decided to try a deflection technique. 'It's my turn!' I burst out. This startled most of the ladies. 'Which box should I pick?' I jumped up to select my gift."

"And?"

"It worked—or at least it seemed to. One of the ladies said, 'Oh, pick that one, the big box in the middle.' I did. Then I tore off the wrapping all in one motion, saying, 'Let me show you how to open a Christmas gift.' This lovely silver platter was inside. Then I quickly asked, 'Who's next?' I wanted to keep things moving, pretending that the whoopee cushion debacle had never even happened."

"What about the whoopee cushion?" I asked.

"Melba casually placed it in her pocket and graciously pretended she was given a whoopee cushion every holiday."

We had a good laugh.

The holiday was a success. Allie enjoyed her treats. She cherished the day of succulent turkey and enjoyed the five-day feast of turkey leftovers.

Some time after the first of the year, Melba Carter came to the clinic for her blood-pressure check.

"Your blood pressure is looking good today, Melba," I told her, and we conversed for a moment. "Oh, I heard you and the SWAMP club ladies had an enjoyable evening the other night."

"Yes, we did," Melba said.

"And how was the gift exchange?" I gently probed.

"Simply wonderful. We had some lovely gifts this year." A curious expression came over her face. "That is, most of us."

I waited cautiously for her to continue.

"That is, except . . ." She hesitated.

"Except what?" I encouraged her.

"Except I received the strangest thing—a thick, red, rubber balloon of some sort."

"Oh?"

"Yes, I think it was some type of pot holder or hot pad. No matter, it was a lovely gift, and we had an enjoyable time."

I pictured the deflated whoopee cushion set on Melba's dining-room table with a hot casserole on it. I laughed to myself, then got back to the medical business at hand.

CHAPTER 16

Another Move: *Gunning for Change*

After announcing to the community that I would be leaving Weston to return to a second residency at Oklahoma State University in Tulsa, Oklahoma, I began to develop "buyer's remorse." Intuitively, and professionally, this seemed the right move, but I had grown very fond of the people and their town. We had several good-bye gatherings, including a reception at the clinic. Many patients made us departing gifts. One family gave me a figurine of a doctor holding a baby he'd just delivered. I was also given a homemade yard sign for the Kansas City Chiefs. One patient even wrote a poem about me.

During our move, Allie was the epitome of strength. She took one more jaunt around the backyard and the empty house, getting in her final sniffs and smells. She marked her territory for the last time, then hopped into the car, sat upon her pillow and looked ahead smiling, as if to say, "Okay, now what? What new adventure lies ahead?" Once again, I realized how much I could learn from her if I would take time to observe and imitate her behavior.

The home we would be renting in Tulsa was in a modest neighborhood. The houses were similar—three-bedroom, two-bath, two-car-garage homes without basements. The location was one mile from the hospital and easily accessible.

Our landlord was Dr. Felmley, an orthopedic surgeon turned landlord who owned fifteen homes in this fifty-house residential area. He had retired from orthopedic surgery a few years before and now rented all of these homes to medical residents. In the fifteen houses of that neighborhood, nearly fifteen different medical specialties were represented.

Dr. Felmley's houses were clean, and the rent was reasonable. He treated the residents fairly and promptly took care of any maintenance needed. We affectionately called the neighborhood Felmley Acres.

My first-year salary as a radiology resident was $27,000. We had taken a fourfold decrease in salary for me to come back to school. Tracy did her best to accept the drop in our standard of living.

Many of the surrounding houses had not been taken care of and showed wear and tear. There were several neglected yards in which the grass had been replaced by overgrown weeds. Several teens dressed in grunge were standing on the street corner, smoking cigarettes.

When we pulled up to our new home and opened the car door, Allie hopped out, sniffed around the yard, marked each corner, then trotted through the front door into the empty house in a manner that said, "Okay, this isn't too bad. In fact, it will do just fine."

Within a week of moving, we began to question the wisdom of my decision. Tracy, Allie and I were jolted awake one night when we heard a loud *kaboom*, then another, and another.

"What's that?" I asked. "It's not . . ."

"Yes, it's gunfire," Tracy said.

We lay there silently. Allie let out a soft growl. The hair on her back bristled. The gunshots continued, fading into the distance. Thankfully, whoever was shooting and whatever their target, they were moving away from us. Tracy fondly referred to our new neighborhood as "Little Beirut," as Lebanon was in the midst of civil war.

Several months of residing in Felmley Acres made it clear that we were living in the worst part of town. Several times a week, we would hear gunshots in the middle of the night. Allie automatically alerted us by growling a second or two before we actually heard the gunfire.

We had never lived in a place with gang warfare, loud domestic squabbles and weapons. We found this constant barrage frightening.

One day at the hospital one of the other residents asked if anyone had heard the gunfire the night before at Felmley Acres. Several of us said yes.

"I have a gun at our house," he said, "and I'll be glad to fill some deviant with buckshot or bullet holes if anyone tries to come into my house."

Nearly thirty years before, I had taken a hunter's safety course, and I had shot a gun only on a few occasions since. I had forgotten a great deal, but while having a healthy respect for firearms, I wasn't afraid of them.

After several discussions and much pondering, Tracy and I decided to get a gun. After all, didn't we have a right to bear arms and protect ourselves? Her willingness to learn to hold, handle, and shoot a gun spoke volumes.

I found a radiology technologist who was skilled at handling a gun. David even had his concealed-weapons license. I asked him for pointers.

"I can do better than that," he said. "I've given firearm-safety instruction and private firearm lessons. I'll be glad to teach you and your wife."

We subsequently purchased a handgun and began to expand our knowledge of firearm safety and to develop shooting skills. At first, Tracy showed an understandable hesitancy, but within two lessons she felt right at home.

Tulsa had a very sophisticated indoor rifle range where they conducted classes for their police academy during the day. At night, the facility was open to members. David was a member and could get us in as his guests. The range had individual firing lanes surrounded by bullet-proof glass. Paper targets of a human torso and head could be mechanically placed at various distances from as close as twenty feet to as far away as three hundred feet.

My mom had always contended that women were better shots than men. She had determined this from her own experiences hunting with her five brothers while growing up, and then confirmed it when hunting with my father after they were married. According to Mom, women have a steadier hand, better eyesight and a gentler pull on the trigger than men. I never knew whether this was a way to one-up my dad or if it was true . . . that was, until now.

Tracy was a natural. I could place five or six shots in close proximity to the targets and manage to hit the torso each time. Tracy, on the other hand, could place her five or six rounds within inches of the target's heart or directly on the skull at the level of the forehead.

I started calling her "Annie Oakley"—a pet name I believe she enjoyed more than many of the more ridiculous terms of endearment I had tried on her over the years. In fact, she got so good at target practice that by the last day she was the star pupil. After plastering her target in the heart and the brain, she asked David if she could keep the paper silhouette—she wants to show all our friends and family what a great shooter she has become, I thought. For obvious reasons, I didn't ask for my paper target after my last rounds.

The next day when I came home from the hospital, I noticed something hanging on our front glass door. When I got close enough, I realized it was her paper target with the bullet holes in perfect placement. Underneath was Tracy's signature in big, red letters. In a second I realized the ingenuity of this simple act. What better deterrent for a potential intruder than to know that the lady of the house owned a gun she wasn't afraid to use, but even more important, that she was an excellent shot? The target remained on our storm door for our entire stay in Tulsa.

Besides my getting a radiology education, we felt it was time to make a full commitment to starting a family. After Tracy's miscarriage, we had assumed the next pregnancy would naturally follow, but here we were two years later, no closer than before to having a baby. Soon an infertility specialist led us down the path to fertility.

Our first assignment was to prove that the problem did not lie with me. "It can't be me," I argued. "Otherwise, Tracy would never have gotten pregnant the first time."

My argument did not carry any weigh, however. "Even though men are under the delusion that their virility translates into powerful sperm, that's not always the case," our doctor said. His directness bruised my ego.

He continued, "Although the problem is usually the female's, there are plausible reasons why the male might be the source of the fertility dilemma. So we should first assess you and your sperm."

Merely discussing my genetic supply suggested to me how much fun having infertility checkups and appointments would be. Not! I dreaded them already.

Allie was more attentive than I expected. If I hugged or kissed Tracy, Allie jumped onto my lap. Her reaction begged the question "why?" I hoped this was her way of showing her support of the whole family idea, but I suspected she was actually envious.

A thorough medical analysis of my genetic donation revealed I was not the problem. Like so many men who have undergone fertility testing, I was relieved my spermatozoa were functioning just fine.

Tracy then began her journey in infertility and was scheduled for a full-body medical workup as a first step. She was given instructions on basal body temperature measurements and a routine ovulatory education.

A hysterosalpingogram was arranged with Dr. Freeman, our OB GYN, who was a subspecialist in fertility. This was a surgical procedure in which the gynecologist inserted a small tube through the cervix into the uterus. He would then forcefully inject a dye into the uterus and through the fallopian tubes to dislodge any blockage within the tubes. In lay terms, I had heard many patients say after a hysterosalpingogram, "the doctor blew out my tubes."

We set the date for surgery. As with most elective surgeries, we were scheduled early in the morning. We were instructed to show up at five forty-five, one hour before the surgery.

The morning came bright and early. Even Allie sensed we were up earlier than usual that day. After caring for Allie's needs and bidding her farewell, we headed for the hospital. Tracy and I arrived promptly at five forty-five, in time to sit in the pre-op holding area and wait for forty-five minutes. I wasn't used to being the family of the patient, and waiting was not my forte. It surprised me how nervous I was. I kept thinking to myself, what if something goes wrong? I kept these thoughts to myself. I did not want to alarm Tracy.

After we completed the check-in and pre-op requirements, Tracy was given a sedative for relaxation. At six forty-five, she was taken back to the operating room, and I was ushered into the waiting room.

About one hour later, Dr. Freeman came through the waiting-room door, "All went well," he said. "I blew out her tubes. Everything looks good. We'll see how things go. Go forth and procreate." Then he was gone.

Following doctor's orders, we started right away, and to our surprise and delight, Tracy missed her next period.

We couldn't believe it would happen so quickly. Only fourteen days after Tracy's fallopian tubes had been forced open, she conceived. After suffering through the miscarriage experience, we vowed not to tell anyone until after the first trimester—for our own sake and the sake of others.

This time things progressed normally. We were extremely excited, but forced caution. Somehow, we thought this would protect us if anything went wrong. To our great pleasure, this pregnancy remained on schedule, and soon we were only weeks away from the big event.

We had both heard or read that some dogs turn against newborns. Sometimes pets become aggressive in a territorial fashion. Although Allie's personality was way too pleasant for us to anticipate this scenario, the possibility of her rejecting the new baby existed.

Several behavioral specialists advise preparing a family pet for the upcoming change in her life. We followed their advice. Several weeks before Tracy's due date, we gave Allie diapers to sniff. We had purchased a baby crib and prepared the nursery. Several times a day we placed Allie in the crib. She sniffed around, then sat on her haunches and looked at us in her own curious way as if to ask, "What kind of game is this?" Her actions caused me to wonder if we were off our rockers.

We had enough practice trips to the hospital in the middle of the night, only to learn the distinct difference between false contractions and full-fledged contractions. I think that I was more embarrassed than Tracy for my failure to detect true labor. Even though Braxton-Hicks (false contractions) are a common reason for early trips to Labor and Delivery, I felt that I should have known the difference. When I was delivering babies, I always cautioned my patients to be wary of false contractions. And yet, when it came to my own wife, I had failed to recognize the difference.

During this educational trip, Allie sat in her cage for several hours until we returned. Even with all of our thought and preparation, we had not planned for a doggie sitter for Allie when Tracy actually went into labor. Like any good practice run, this labor drill had enabled us the opportunity to fine-tune our plan. We arranged for a future Allie sitter. We still had time to get Allie used to the idea of a new baby in our home. For that matter, Tracy and I had a little more time to get used to the idea, too.

It was difficult to fully comprehend how much our lives would change. Was any parent, father or furry sister ever ready for this life-altering event? Trying to be good "doggy parents," we continued to simulate life with a newborn. Little did we realize this was mighty tough to simulate or practice.

Allie was now eight years old, and I had just turned thirty-five. We weren't too old to learn something new, were we? We were about to find out.

Chapter 17

A Child Is Born: *Allie as Big Sister*

One of our next-door neighbors in Tulsa had a Boxer, with whom Allie had a strained relationship. Allie barked and bellowed at the Boxer like she was twice his size. The Boxer would charge at the common fence and then run back and forth, growling, barking and pawing at the ground. This behavior provoked Allie. She stiffened her hind legs, arched her back and barked. Each time she barked, her hind legs and buttocks raised off the ground in a comical fashion. The Boxer seemed intrigued with this stance and revved up his engine even more, which only riled Allie further.

On January 21, 1999, around nine P.M., I turned on the back light and went to the backyard with Allie. The Boxer was outside, too. There was a stiff Arctic wind from the north and a tiny amount of moisture in the air. The weatherman had predicted snow. The two dogs forgot about the cold and commenced to antagonize one another. But without my coat, I began to shiver within a couple minutes. "You know, you two," I spoke to Allie and her adversary, "it's too cold to be carrying on like this. Go inside." Allie gave a final emphatic bark, then turned with a hrrumppff, and pranced inside.

Allie went right to the laundry room, where Tracy was measuring detergent to run a load of my medical scrubs. Allie had grown fond of dirty laundry.

"You know," I said to Tracy, "She's always liked lying on our piles of dirty clothing, but this is different. See how she takes great effort in forming a pile? She's been at it for five minutes."

"Yes, she's nesting," Tracy said matter-of-factly.

"Nesting?"

"Yes, her motherly instincts cause her to think she's pregnant right along with me, just like the first time I was pregnant."

"You don't believe that?" I asked.

"Sure, she's been doing this for nearly a week, but it's more pronounced lately."

"Really? Maybe she knows something we don't."

Around one thirty A.M. Tracy nudged me. "Kipp, it's time."

I was instantly awake. "How do you know?"

"I didn't want to say anything before in case of another false alarm, but I've been having contractions for the past two to three hours, and they are now every ten minutes and lasting thirty to forty seconds."

"Is this like the last time?" I remained skeptical.

"Nope, these are much harder."

Her inflection was convincing. Like a well-orchestrated fire drill, we performed our assigned duties. I called one of our friends who had agreed to come and stay with Allie, then Tracy and I headed out the door.

Hundreds of contractions later, and after an outpouring of blood, sweat, and tears, the moment arrived. At six twenty-eight A.M. on January 22, 1999, Kolby Gavin Van Camp entered this world, weighing in at seven pounds, fourteen ounces, and measuring twenty-one inches long.

During this experience, I developed a new respect and appreciation for the OB/GYN from the father's point of view. Kolby's delivery was difficult, requiring suction-extraction, and ultimately a forceps delivery, but all ended well for both mother and child. We welcomed a healthy, happy baby into this world. Within hours, Tracy began to implement her predetermined child-rearing schedule, following to the letter the advice of *On Becoming Baby Wise,* a book about a pediatrician's theories on infant care and early childhood training.

By the end of the second day, Tracy and Kolby were released from the hospital. I loaded Kolby into the car seat, then assisted Tracy into the car, and we drove home. Everything seemed all too familiar that morning when we left the hospital, yet instinctively, we knew everything had changed forever, in ways we couldn't yet even imagine.

Kimberly, Tracy's sister, had come to help us with the new baby. She had the garage door open, awaiting our arrival. The weatherman had accurately predicted the one inch of snow now covering the ground.

"I want to get Allie and show her the baby before we bring him inside," I said. "I hope she likes him and isn't aggressive or territorial."

"I think she'll be just fine," Tracy said.

I lifted Allie into the backseat and pulled the blanket away from the carrier. There lay baby Kolby, sleeping and content. Allie peered into the car seat, then pushed her nose up toward Kolby's face. I held her back to keep her from getting too close. I stood cautiously by, eyeing her every move while she sniffed for several seconds, then licked his little hands. Finally, she hopped down from the car onto the garage floor.

Kimberly assisted Tracy while I picked up Kolby in his carrier. Allie stayed at my side, sniffing toward the carrier and Kolby while we went into the living room.

I sat the car seat down, and Allie pushed her nose through the blanket as if to say, "Let me get a good sniff at him." Kolby was wrapped up like a bug in its cocoon. We lifted him from the car seat and lowered him onto a blanket in the middle of the floor. I gently restrained Allie to keep her from getting too close. Thus far, she had shown only appropriate curiosity, but I didn't want to give her any chance to reject Kolby.

My fears were unfounded. Allie was the perfect older sister. She showed instant love and interest in Kolby. She loved his many different smells, especially his dirty diapers. She proved to be his fierce protector. She confirmed what we had always known: She had a heart of gold and was incapable of hatred or disdain for any member of our family.

Allie was more gentle with Kolby than I remembered her ever being with anyone else. She seemed to be smiling just as much as we were.

I leaned back against the couch, soaking in the unforgettable moment. When Allie came along, we became a family, but now with Kolby, all seemed complete.

I broke the blissful silence. "I guess I shouldn't have been so worried. Allie acts like she knows more about newborns than we do."

Allie wagged her tail, and her body wagged along. She snuggled against Kolby and curled up next to him on his blanket.

"Looks like he's a keeper," I said. And at that moment, all was right with the world.

CHAPTER 18

Runaway Stroller: *Allie's off and Racing*

Tracy had become a stay-at-home mom when we moved to Tulsa, a role that suited her well. She was able to devote all of her attention to her family. Having Tracy around all day was pleasing to Allie, too.

After Kolby was born, Tracy made a conscious effort to get back to her pre-pregnancy weight. She loaded the stroller, Kolby, and Allie into the car and headed to the Arkansas River, where there were numerous walking trails.

Allie loved her daily walk. The first thirty minutes found her olfactory lobe on overload. She wanted to get a careful whiff of literally thousands of unique smells. But Tracy wasn't there to entertain Allie; she had her own goal to achieve. She was driven, and Allie was determined. Not a week went by that Allie didn't cause some type of excitement. Of the many dogs walking along the river, Allie always thought she was the alpha dog. It didn't matter how big or what the breed, Allie was always on alert to inform her adversary that she was in charge.

One afternoon Tracy placed Kolby in the stroller, hooked Allie to her leash and attached the leash to the stroller. Then Tracy leaned into the car to get her radio and headset. At that moment, Allie caught sight of a dog trotting along the river thirty to forty feet away.

In a flash, she was off, eight-month-old Kolby in tow. Seeing Kolby and the stroller headed down the walking trail, Tracy frantically charged after the stroller as it sped along the bumpy path. Allie raced ahead like the lead husky of a dog-sled team competing in the Iditerod. Reaching a bend in the path, she took a sharp turn to the left. The stroller stayed on the direct course.

Just when tragedy seemed inevitable, Tracy caught the stroller and jerked it to a halt. Allie's adventure came to an abrupt stop. The taut leash pulled her off her feet.

Tracy lifted the stroller cover to assess any harm to Kolby. His feet and arms were flailing in the air, and he was laughing—that unique and infectious laugh we had already grown to love. He'd enjoyed the entire escapade.

This had been a joy ride through the park for our son. After her initial fear subsided, Tracy found his amusement infectious. She started laughing.

With everything back in order, they began their walk, this time in their more predictable, controlled fashion. By the time they reached the half-mile mark, Allie was panting heavily. Her prance had slowed to a walk, and soon she plopped down on her belly with her hind legs sprawled behind her, refusing to go any farther.

After coaxing her for several minutes Tracy decided to pick up and carry her. But carrying a twelve-pound dog was no easy task. After a moment of deliberation, Tracy put Allie in the stroller next to Kolby. Soon Allie settled down and snuggled next to Kolby. True to form, despite all these obstacles, Tracy completed her exercise that afternoon.

As the days got warmer, Allie reached her level of exhaustion around the one-mile mark. Tracy simply stuck Allie into the stroller with Kolby. On several occasions, people would stop and ask if they could get a peek at the baby. Tracy enjoyed the surprised looks when the stranger glanced over the side of the stroller to see Allie and Kolby side-by-side.

One quick-witted lady said, "Oh, I see the resemblance. The hairy one must be from your side, and the little boy must look more like your husband."

One afternoon several weeks later, Tracy was preoccupied, listening to talk radio and Rush Limbaugh, and did not pick up on Allie's blatant signs of exhaustion. But Allie solved the matter herself, hopping into the bottom compartment of the stroller.

From that day forward, when Allie was finished with her walk, she jumped into the lower level of the double-decker stroller and rode like a queen throughout the rest of the park. This new perch became Allie's personal royal carriage with Tracy as the driver.

Allie had found yet another way to control Tracy and me. Transporting her around the park in her noble chariot was simply one more job we could perform on her behalf.

CHAPTER 19

Allie's Warning: *Weathering the Storms*

Occasionally, post-graduate residents are required to travel to another part of the country for additional training. For example, the hospital where I completed my diagnostic radiology residency in Tulsa was not a children's medical facility, so I completed the pediatric training of my radiology residency at highly regarded children's hospitals around the country.

I spent three months at Children's Mercy in Kansas City, Missouri; the Children's Hospital in Denver, Colorado; and Children's Hospital in Columbus, Ohio. I also had to spend six weeks at the American Armed Forces Institute of Pathology in Washington, D.C., at Walter Reed Medical Center.

I chose to fulfill this requirement during the spring of my junior year. Kolby was only a few months old at that time. In April 1999, I packed my car, bade my wife, son, and furry daughter farewell and headed east.

When I arrived in Washington sixteen hours later, I located my accommodations. The house where I would rent a room for the next six weeks was only two blocks from Walter Reed. I could walk to the base each day. The Armed Forces Institute of Pathology, AFIP, had assisted radiology residents with their training for about thirty years. Their program was highly organized and extremely informative. I had access to the medical facility at the base, and I had the opportunity to use the commissary as well as the gymnasium and workout facilities.

My schedule was full. I walked to Walter Reed every day with two other residents who were renting rooms in the same house. The courses began at seven each morning. After five hours of lectures from top-notch authorities from around the nation and the world, we had a one-hour lunch break.

I generally ate at the cafeteria at Walter Reed Hospital, where soldiers who had been injured in combat were recovering and rehabilitating from all kinds of war injuries. It was common to sit down and eat lunch with a different war vet every day. The lectures resumed at one P.M. and lasted until four. From four to five was an informal review. I often skipped the case review sessions and headed to the exercise facility, where I could get in an hour workout.

Ten days after I left, Tracy, Kolby and Allie drove to Kansas City to attend a baby shower for Kolby, given by our friends in Weston and Kansas City. It was storming when Tracy got back to Tulsa. She had just traveled five hours with a baby and a dog, and although she had grown accustomed to my absence, the solo trip had worn her out.

Upon arriving home and pulling into the garage, Allie refused to get out of the car. Allie's unwillingness to cooperate irritated Tracy. Not only did Allie refuse to get out of the vehicle, after Tracy carried her into the house, she refused to go outside into the backyard. Instead, she stood at the door and barked—a highly unusual behavior for her. Trying to coax Allie to go outside, Tracy went out into the backyard, where she realized that the storm was much worse than she had initially thought.

I'd just fallen asleep after a long day of training and lectures, when the phone jarred me awake around eleven P.M. The tone in Tracy's voice alerted me that something was amiss.

"A tornado is heading straight up the Oklahoma Turnpike. It's about twenty miles from us," she said.

Having grown up in Kansas, I knew plenty about tornadoes. When we moved to Oklahoma, I was amazed that most houses did not have basements. The residents were living in Tornado Alley but had few methods of protecting themselves.

"I'm heading over to John and Lisa's to stay in their basement," Tracy said. These friends were the only people we knew in Tulsa who had a basement.

"How bad is it?" I asked.

"The weatherman said it's approaching a mile wide."

"You better get going, pronto. Call me when you get there," I said and hung up.

Now wide awake, I turned on the Weather Channel. It was reporting tornadoes in the Midwest, but nothing out of the ordinary for the time of the year.

About thirty minutes later, I received Tracy's call. "We're here," she said. "It's a bad one!"

I could hear the tornado sirens in the background. "How are Kolby and Allie?"

"Kolby's asleep in his car seat. He was awake while I loaded him in the pickup; he probably thought this was an adventure."

"In a way it is," I said. "How about Allie?"

"I think she knew something was wrong. She was acting strangely this evening."

"In what way?"

"Restless. Maybe she could sense danger in the air."

That didn't surprise me. Over the years, Allie had found many ways to communicate danger, and this was no exception.

"You still have an interest in storm chasing?" I asked Tracy. For some unusual reason, she had a longtime interest in following severe storms closely.

"I'm not sure," she answered. "This one really scared me. Our flimsy little home didn't make me feel safe. The wind was so strong, I swore the roof was about to blow off."

"Well, you're safe now. I'll talk to you in the morning."

My alarm went off early the next morning. It was five A.M. in the Midwest, and I knew if anything had gone wrong, Tracy would have let me know.

Upon completing the morning session, I decided to skip lunch and work out at the gym. After five minutes on the treadmill, a TV tuned to CNN flashed across the bottom of the screen, "Coming up next, F5 tornado devastates Oklahoma."

I listened closely.

"From Oklahoma City to Tulsa, Oklahoma residents had a restless night as F5, 1.5 mile-wide tornado wreaked havoc on their cities and state. The area has been declared a national disaster, and the early estimates of damage were 220 million dollars."

The first photograph showed a U-shaped strip mall with about ten stores. The second picture showed nothing but a cement slab. The strip mall had been destroyed and blown away. Upon studying the picture closely, I recognized the mall. It was only twenty miles from our home. We had shopped there before.

The sight of the demolished mall alarmed me. Even though Tracy had described the storm, it really hadn't registered just how destructive this tornado had been, until I saw those pictures.

I called Tracy. "Everyone okay?"

"Everyone in our family is." She sounded sad. "But lots of people have had their home turned up-side-down. Many houses were destroyed."

"How about our home?"

"Part of the fence blew down," she said.

"Sounds like we were pretty lucky."

I found out later that the tornado had twisted and weaved randomly up the Will Rogers turnpike. We lived one quarter of a mile off the turnpike. Fortunately, the Tasmanian-like wind devil had lifted back into the clouds about two blocks short of our neighborhood, or we might have lost everything.

Allie had sensed that a twister was coming directly at us. Thanks to her and thanks to the grace of God, my family and our home survived an F5 tornado and lived to tell about it.

CHAPTER 20

Allie Meets an Alley Cat

Dogs have always played a unique role in my family's lives. Growing up, we had a long list of pets. First was Lady, the Miniature Collie, who wandered into our yard one day. She liked what she saw and who she met, so she adopted us. She became a wonderful pet, whose kind spirit was perfect for four young kids—my brother, two sisters, and me.

Also, Mom and Dad brought numerous stray animals home from Dad's veterinary clinic. These included all types of pets—from rabbits to dogs and cats, turtles, talking parrots, and parakeets. The most unusual and exotic pets enhanced our standing with the neighbor kids. One of the most unique was Paca, the ferret. It became a running joke at school and throughout our neighborhood; what type of animal is that? Is it your new pet?

Each dog in my family was treated more like a person than a dog. It started with my sister Kim's Mimi, a Toy Poodle. She was one of my favorite pets, who, like Allie, arrived on Christmas morning, only fifteen years earlier. Even though Mimi was Kim's pet, she had a special influence on me. Mimi was the first pet that taught me about the close bond that can develop between humans and their pets. Besides observing the closeness that Kim felt towards Mimi, I felt a tight bond with Allie. This was my first memory of how a pet could effect my feelings on such a deep level.

I have seen Mimi in Allie many times over the years. I suspect this is because of the close bond I felt towards Mimi as a young man. Allie and Mimi had similar personalities. Both were highly intelligent and independent and filled our lives with excitement and entertainment.

Mimi was a master thief. She could locate any candy in the house and manage to steal it when no one was looking. One day Mimi found an entire bag of miniature Snickers, and when Kim discovered Mimi on her bed, she was devouring the last bar. Her white muzzle was covered in chocolate, and her pink belly was more protuberant than usual.

Though Allie and Mimi never knew each other, they were kindred spirits. During residency I had been given a bag of Three Musketeers for my birthday from one of the radiology technologists. I had placed it in a duffle bag I carried back and forth to work. One day I heard some rustling in the closet in our bedroom. I cautiously opened the door only to see my duffle bag moving with sounds of rooting and rustling of paper. When I pulled back the opening, there was Allie looking up at me with a half-eaten Three Musketeers candy bar in her mouth. Her face was covered in chocolate, a strong contrast to her white fur.

After Mimi died, Kim located another Poodle, as did Mom and Dad. The two Poodles were Teacup Poodles, and they were sisters. Teacups, also known as Pocket Poodles, are the tiniest variety of the breed, usually weighing less than four pounds. Mom and Dad had a small Phantom Poodle named Snookie, which was short for Babee Snookums. Kim's Apricot Teacup was named Kupid. Being kin, Snookie and Kupid spent much of their lives together.

When Allie arrived on the scene, Snookie and Kupid were about ten years old, and they saw no reason to accept a new puppy into the family, especially one that had grown to three times their size. When the dogs were together, Snookie and Kupid made it very clear to Allie that they were the canine matriarchs of the family and that she was to keep her place. But Allie was not intimidated. She tried desperately to get them to play with her, barking, wagging her tail, nipping at their heels and sniffing their backsides, but to no avail.

Another family pet was Tommy, my sister Keli's black-haired Shih Tzu. Tommy and Allie were puppies together and formed a special bond when they arrived on the scene in 1991. Tommy lived with his family in Colorado. Whenever our families returned to our parents in Colby for vacations, Tommy and Allie had their own reunion of sorts. Many evenings the two youthful dogs showed the matriarchal canine cousins how to play. One of their favorite activities was chasing each other nonstop around the furniture. Bichons are quicker on their feet than Shih Tzus, and poor Tommy's tongue hung to the floor within minutes of starting their chase, in spite of his training in the high altitude of the Rockies.

One summer, when Allie was nine years old, we went to Colby for a week's stay. Mom and Dad had a pool in their backyard, and we spent much of our time swimming. The day after we arrived, I let Allie out into the fenced in backyard to explore. She meandered around for a few minutes, sniffing all the new odors.

Suddenly, I heard a blood-curdling canine shriek. Tracy and I bolted outside. Allie's ears lay flat back, and she was darting toward the door with her tail between her legs, all the while letting out a sound I had never heard her make before.

"What's wrong, Allie?" I asked as she cowered between my legs.

Chester, a long-haired Persian alley cat that Mom and Dad had rescued and adopted as their own, sat on the swing next to the pool. He was my dad's favorite cat. He was still hissing, and the hair on his tail stood on end.

Suddenly, Tracy and I both realized Allie had never seen a cat before.

"Are you afraid of Chester?" I asked Allie.

Her answer was unmistakable: She looked up at me with eyes filled with terror. I picked her up. "Poor Allie. Let's go meet Chester. You'll see, he's really harmless."

I then carried Allie over to the swing where Chester was sitting. When I reached out to pet Chester, he purred. Allie squirmed in my arms. She finally managed to wiggle free. Chester let out a meow and another hiss, and Allie escaped while making the same high-pitched scream, her tail between her legs and ears pinned back as she darted toward the screen door. I went after her.

"Well, Allie," I said, picking her up. "I didn't know you were afraid of cats. Does mean old Chester scare you? And you've always acted so tough."

I'd always thought cats were supposed to be scared of dogs, not the other way around.

CHAPTER *21*

Making the Transition: *Saying Good-Bye to Family Pets*

During my final year of radiology residency, Snookie and Kupid both aged rapidly. Each time I saw them, they had grown more frail. In the last year Snookie had gone blind, was deaf, and barely ate enough to sustain life. To observe the natural decline of Snookie, who only yesterday seemed youthful and lively, triggered my thoughts regarding our Allie. A languid emptiness enveloped my mind. How would I deal with this? I only entertained this notion for a moment. Afterall, she was only ten.

The college football team my family followed had made it to the Fiesta Bowl, and everyone, except my sister Kim and her husband, Lynn, was going to the game. Kim and Lynn agreed to take care of Snookie for Mom and Dad. I knew Mom had some trepidation leaving as she feared the worst—Snookie could die while Mom was away.

Throughout the week we were gone, Kim gave Mom daily updates. Snookie was teetering between survival and giving up the ghost. Some days were better than others. I could see the worry on Mom's face with each phone call.

My parents taught us kids early about our responsibility to our domesticated pets. When the time came, it was up to us to put them down to end their suffering.

As a doctor, I found myself reflecting that man would not allow a pet to suffer but would use every heroic method to keep loved ones alive with machines and medical techniques. The dichotomy was extreme.

After the football game, our family split up to travel home. Dad stayed with the rest of the family and enjoyed a more leisurely trip home. I raced ahead with Mom in hopes she could be with Snookie in her final days and hours. After a seventeen-hour whirlwind drive across the midwestern United States, we arrived at my sister's home around three o'clock on Friday afternoon.

Snookie was still alive. We had made it. In fact, she even showed a brief moment of rallying and knew who Mom was. Snookie lifted her head from her deathbed, wagged her tail and licked Mom's hand—a heart-wrenching reunion.

For the next couple of hours, Snookie rested peacefully in Mom's arms, but everything changed in an instant. Snookie suddenly became restless and opened her mouth wide. A loud pop could be heard across the room, then a whimper. The sound was similar to that created by snapping a chicken bone in two.

"What happened?" I asked Mom.

"I don't know." The concern in her voice was obvious.

For several minutes we examined Snookie, feeling her mouth and jaw, opening and closing her mouth, examining her jaw bone, and evaluating the joint of her mouth. Although I couldn't detect any deformity, I couldn't help thinking that perhaps she had broken her jaw.

We engaged in one of those dreaded conversations. "Mom," I asked, "do you think it's time?"

After a long pause, Mom answered hesitantly, "Yes, I think it is."

I tried to console her. "What an incredible will to live. Look how she has hung on this last week, just waiting for you to come home."

I was amazed at the depth of feelings that a person can have for a pet. This human-animal bond was stronger than many human-human bonds I had observed. I was impressed with Snookie's determination to hang on until Mom returned to her side. Seeing the love and affection that Mom and Snookie felt towards each other touched me deeply. I recognized the feelings; they were the same ones I had for Allie.

Kim called her vet, who agreed to meet us at the animal clinic. I offered to take Snookie, but Mom declined my offer. She knew she needed to be present to comfort Snookie in her final moments.

Dr. Smith was already at the clinic when we arrived. He ushered us into one of the examination rooms, where Snookie was placed upon the table. As the son of a veterinarian, I had assisted with countless euthanasias, and none of them was easy.

The doctor accessed a vein on his first attempt, for which I was grateful. Dr. Smith injected the deadly toxin into Snookie's veins, and, with the room eerily silent, Snookie slightly raised her head and licked Mom's hand as if to say, "It's okay, I'm ready to go." The pet consoled the master. Snookie breathed her last breath around five thirty P.M. on January 3. In some simple way, Snookie's display of unconditional love provided Mom the solace and comfort she needed to get through the day.

Witnessing this caused my mind to race forward to that inevitable day we would face with Allie. These thoughts chilled my heart, and I quickly forced them from my mind.

Mom had a small pet tombstone engraved, which is still in her garden. When Mom and Dad moved from Colby to Topeka several years later to be closer to family, they brought the placard with them, a constant reminder of yet another pet who had touched our lives.

The loss of Snookie wasn't only difficult for Mom and my family. It was also hard on her sister, Kupid. The night after we put Snookie down, Kupid was restless, an uncharacteristic behavior for her, especially when she was in her own home and familiar surroundings. Kupid seemed to know what had happened; she missed her sister.

Not long after Snookie was put down, Kim and Lynn went on a weeklong trip of their own. Tracy and I agreed to watch Kupid. She'd always been somewhat high strung when away from her home or when Kim and Lynn were gone. I now understood what Kim and Lynn had gone through with Snookie. This time, Tracy and I were watching a frail, geriatric canine, all the while wondering if she would survive the week. Fortunately, she did.

On multiple occasions over the next several months, Kim called and said, "I think it's about time to put Kupid down." Yet as soon as she had uttered those words, Kupid would rebound, showing an undying spirit and will to live.

On a Tuesday morning in the middle of spring, Kim called. "This is the day. I think Kupid is suffering."

"Do you want me to come up?" I asked. Tulsa was four hours south of Salina, where Kim and Lynn lived.

"Only if you can. That's up to you."

Now, I knew I couldn't go to the radiology resident program director and say, "My sister has to put her dog to sleep. I'd like the day off." Instead, I called Dr. George Erbacher and said, "My aunt, who lives in Salina, is on her deathbed. I'd like to try and get there before she passes on."

George gave his permission for me to miss a day of work.

Not until Allie died did I realize exactly what Kim had been going through—the torture of watching the clock, knowing as each minute passed that Kupid was one minute closer to the end. It was dreadful, like a person on death row must feel after the execution date is set.

I arrived around twelve forty-five. Kim and Lynn had an appointment with their veterinarian, Dr. Smith at one thirty. As we had done only six months before with Snookie, we drove to the vet's office. Kim was too distraught to go in, so Lynn and I went into the animal clinic together. Lynn, too, had grown to love Kupid, but I never really realized until that moment just how hard this would be on him.

Lynn consoled Kupid while the doctor accessed her vein. The entire scene was surreal, as we had recently gone through this, in this very room. I was astonished as I observed the same behavior from Kupid that I had witnessed from Snookie. She lifted her head slightly off the blanket and licked Lynn's hands. Once again the pet consoled the master.

Kupid had outlived all the other dogs in our family's long history of pets. She died at the ripe old age of fifteen and a half, about one hundred and eight in human years. I had once more been present to observe and participate in the most important decision a master makes for his pet.

CHAPTER 22

Radiology Calls: *A Capitol Move*

At about the time we had settled and grown accustomed to Tulsa, I was on the brink of my final year of radiology residency. I was thirty-eight years old and still going to school. Even though I was tired of medical training and did not relish the thought of another year of education, I knew I needed to seriously consider doing a fellowship, sub-specialty training might be the best method of providing job security.

If I was to engage in a final year of medical training, it would need to immediately follow the residency. So I began applying for fellowships in interventional radiology, a subspecialty of general radiology where radiologists use x-ray guidance to perform minimally invasive, surgical procedures.

I was intrigued by the Interventional Radiology Fellowship at the Washington Hospital Center in Washington, D.C. The program director, Dr. Richard Gray, had personally responded to my inquiry and laid out his ideas for the direction of the fellowship program. A visionary, his focus on clinical radiology was well ahead of the current trend in radiology at that time. He was looking for a candidate with experience in general medicine, and with my background in family practice, I was a natural fit.

I accepted the fellowship, and my senior year of residency passed quickly.

Before we knew it, yet another moving day had arrived. Allie hopped into the car and curled upon the basket of clothes in the backseat next to Kolby. Her demeanor was calm. Kolby, now eighteen months old, smiled and stared out the window, prepared for another adventure. As we drove out of town, neither of them ever looked back.

On the way, we stopped in St. Louis to see Tracy's parents. When we turned off the interstate to head to their home, Allie knew where she was. She jumped into the front seat and crawled over me to get to the window. The closer we got, the more Allie carried on. She started out whimpering, progressed to guttural moaning and ultimately let out a shrill bark as we rounded the final corner, her own exclamation point upon this leg of the trip.

Not surprisingly, Allie was the first one out of the car. She darted into the yard and began sniffing. She was happy to be back in familiar surroundings. But as she meandered up to the front stoop, a large, hairy face suddenly appeared at the door. It was Pippin, Tracy's parents' German Shepherd. Pippin hated Allie, and Allie loved to torment Pippin. Allie was visibly startled. Her sympathetic nervous system calmed quickly, and she began to bark and scratch at the storm door. This evoked a similar response from Pippin. Only the glass stood between them and a major dog fight.

The commotion was so loud that even John, Tracy's dad, came to the door to see what was going on. After a game of cat and mouse, Allie and Pippin settled down.

After enjoying a brief stay in St. Louis, we continued our journey to the East Coast. We arrived in the wee hours of a Saturday night in late June 2000. Allie had now been in seventeen states.

We didn't need long to feel at home in our new apartment in Bowie,

Maryland, outside Washington. We quickly made friends. Everything we needed was within a mile of our apartment. Several grocery stores, many convenience stores, any restaurant we desired, and even a minor league baseball team were just around the corner. And then, the thrill of being near our nation's capital and all the treasured landmarks never grew old.

After a few weeks, we sought out a church to attend. One Sunday we pulled into the church parking lot and parked our pickup. As we were getting out of the car, a petite, silver-haired lady came up to us and asked, "Is that a Kansas State University license plate?"

"Why, yes," I said proudly.

"I graduated from K-State in 1949," she responded.

"You're kidding," I said. "Are you from Kansas?"

"I am. I was born and raised in Concordia, and my husband, Vernon, is from a small town in western Kansas," she said.

"Really? Which town?" I asked.

"You probably haven't heard of it," she said. "My husband is Captain Vernon Klemm, born in Colby, Kansas, and later went on to Annapolis, to the U.S. Naval Academy."

"No way!" I exclaimed. "I was born and raised in Colby! That's unbelievable!"

The old saying "It's a small world" was entirely true. What were the odds that one of the first couples we met in Washington would be from Kansas, not to mention my hometown—and a K-State graduate to boot?

Despite the age difference, we developed a lasting friendship with the Klemms. After leaving Washington we stayed in touch. Norene and Vernon made two trips back to Kansas, staying with us on both occasions. On one trip, we took the Klemms to a K-State vs. KU football game. We enjoyed the time we spent with this endearing couple, who had graciously adopted us during those fifty-eight weeks in Washington.

Captain Klemm died of kidney cancer several years later. He was honored for his years of military service and was buried at Arlington

National Cemetery. In November 2005, we flew back to Washington, D.C., for Vernon's ceremonial military burial. It was a once-in-a-life-time experience that we couldn't pass up.

Captain Klemm received the respect befitting a man who served his country for his entire life, fighting to uphold honor and freedom through four major wars.

CHAPTER 23

A Thwarted Attack: *Kipp to the Rescue*

At ten years of age, Allie had an air of confidence about her. Some might even mistake her independence for arrogance. Of course, this noble manner had been bred into her genetic code. A look at her ancestry reminded us that the Bichon Frise had been reared for the sole purpose of providing companionship for the king and queen of France.

After we moved into our apartment complex in Bowie, Maryland, I again took up the routine of taking Allie outside for her nightly constitutional. She had spent much of her life demanding that this be a major production. Allie picked up right where we had left off in Tulsa. She had determined it was my duty to walk her, so on most nights I grabbed the leash, and Allie and I strolled around the square, just the two of us.

The complex consisted of rows of four different buildings, with the one-, two- and three-bedroom apartments positioned in a square. In the center of these buildings was a grass courtyard with flowers, trees and a few bushes. Most of the apartment balconies faced the courtyard, and around the outer perimeter of the each group of buildings was a sidewalk that formed a perfect square. One trip around the outside of this square equaled one trip around a block.

On a good night, Allie required only one trip around the block to locate the precise spot that suited her fancy. On a difficult night, she needed two trips around the block. Occasionally, it took three trips around the block, if she decided to relieve herself at all.

Within a couple of days, she had determined which patch of grass warranted her time and liquid donation. She could squeeze a few drops from her bladder on command, and generally speaking, she watered seven or eight plants with each trip around the block.

Unlike in Tulsa, we now had to keep Allie on a tight lead. The apartment complex was next to a crowded four-lane highway with constant traffic flying up and down the road. There were many distractions to entice her. If she got loose and ran out into the busy street, she would likely be struck by a moving vehicle.

She recognized people and places by their odor. I have always been amazed at the powerful nature of a dog's sense of smell. Allie could recognize other dogs by their deposits along the sidewalk. She perked up whenever she identified a new smell.

One chilly fall afternoon at four, Allie and I were walking around the block. Near the halfway mark, I decided to cut Allie's walk short. The wind had picked up and had a strong bite as it slapped me directly in the face. Allie was unfazed by the cooler temperature but became upset by my decision to call it quits for the day. She had many more smells and spots to check out.

Though she did not speak English, Allie had a distinct method of communicating. Rarely was her personal desire or thought lost in translation.

"Come on, Allie, let's go," I said.

She reluctantly acknowledged me with her eyes, but her nose remained buried in a patch of grass.

"Come on, let's go." I gently tugged on the lead.

She lifted her nose from the grass. Her snout was covered with loose blades of grass and a small amount of dirt. She then deliberately placed her nose smack dab into the middle of the same patch of grass in a defiant fashion.

Her expression was comical, and I found myself smiling, while getting increasingly more frustrated. I waited impatiently for a few seconds, then stated firmly, "Okay, that's it. Let's go."

Her body did not move an inch. I tugged on her leash, which startled her and caught her off balance. She dug in, man versus beast. I tugged harder and spoke louder, my jaw clenched.

Allie sat on her bottom, stuck both her legs out in front, and dug in as if she were the anchor of a rope pull. She even pursed her lips. Her next action surprised me; she turned her upper lip up and showed her teeth.

"Don't you act like that, young lady," I chastised her and began to drag her across the lawn. The last time I had seen this behavior was at the Kennelwise Puppy School, when the obedience-class instructor pulled our unruly little Bichon along the ground.

Because of our personalities, neither man nor beast would easily give in. I tugged, she slid. I pulled, she resisted. I had cut through the back courtyard in the center of our apartment complex, covering about one third of the yard diagonally.

I was about to give in, when a blur of black and white fur caught my peripheral vision. Before I could determine what was going on, a large Dalmatian charged at Allie. Allie yanked on her lead, and the sudden jerk nearly pulled the leash from my hand.

I struggled to pick Allie up while she lunged forward at the approaching foe. She braced herself for a full-fledged canine fight, which made it difficult to restrain her. The Dalmatian growled and snapped at Allie while I jerked her away. Fifteen-pound Allie dangled from her lead, visibly choking and fighting, while I fended off the aggressive Dalmatian, using my own body as a shield. Out of the corner of my eye, I saw the Dalmation's owner sauntering towards us.

I managed to lift Allie to safety at the exact moment that the Dalmatian jumped and sank his teeth into her erect tail. Her yelp, and my disgust with the owner and his dog, triggered an unexpected reaction from me. I banged the palm of my free hand directly on the Dalmatian's head.

This stunned him for a second, which enabled our escape. But he quickly resumed his attack, growling, barking, and leaping toward us. Finally, the Dalmatian's owner arrived and nonchalantly hooked the leash to the collar of his high-strung pet. Allie, shaken, trembled and whimpered.

"You have to keep that beast under control!" I yelled back to the Dalmatian owner. "He almost killed my dog!"

The owner appeared unaffected by my reprimand, as if this was a common event. Maybe it was.

"There are leash laws here!" I yelled louder while I rushed my injured little girl to safety.

The bright-red blood on Allie's snow-white fur gave the appearance that she was bleeding to death. I saw a large gash in her skin, on her buttocks, and much blood on her tail. I gently placed my hand down over the bleeding flesh wound on her tail and raced directly toward the apartment.

When I burst into the apartment with Allie wrapped in my arms, the commotion startled Tracy. I handed Allie off to Tracy and began a thorough examination while angrily recounting the gory details of the encounter. Allie continued to shake. I probed and brushed her fur to the side in an attempt to expose her skin while I continued my examination. She had two flesh wounds, one on her tail and one on her bottom, near her flank. The wound on her rump was the deeper. The wound on her tail was an abrasion.

"She could have died," I said. "Really, if I hadn't been able to tug her out of reach, she could have died. If that first bite had landed on her neck, it would have snapped her neck in two."

The seriousness of this encounter was setting in. Allie sensed our grave concern and jumped right into the conversation. She whimpered.

She looked up at me and whined and whimpered. The concern and fear in my voice fed right into her narcissism. She sensed my worry and put her own exclamation upon it. She began to shake and shiver violently. This triggered more sympathy from us. She ate up the attention.

"Poor Allie," I crooned, stroking her back as we cleaned up her wounds. She whined each time I stroked her. This went on for a few minutes, then she began to relax. So did we.

She did not need any stitches. I was able to close the wounds with steri-strips. She had dodged a major catastrophe. For the rest of our walks during our stay in Bowie, we kept a close lookout for the obstreperous Dalmatian. Allie had a complete recovery in a few days.

CHAPTER 24

The Presidential Treatment: *Sniffing out the Top Dogs*

While in the Washington, D.C., area, our goal was to see as many of the historic sites as possible. Nearly every Saturday, we planned an outing to one or more of the national landmarks. We got to see more national treasures in one year than most people see in a lifetime. During that year, Allie walked up and down the Mall, around the outside of the White House, along the burial grounds of Gettysburg, and even around Thomas Jefferson's home, Monticello.

Kolby was now two years old. I figured he wouldn't remember any of these sites, but still wanted to show him as many national treasures as possible. We enjoyed some interesting and unusual events. Wherever we went, we always brought a camera. Many of these pictures could serve as evidence of Kolby's experiences in D.C. If he ever wanted proof that he was on the steps of the U.S. Capitol the day of the inauguration of George W. Bush, we could produce the photo.

At the Washington Hospital Center, one of the radiology technologists was engaged to marry a young man in the White House Secret

Service. One day in the winter of 2000, Delaina asked me if Tracy, Kolby, and I had any interest in seeing the White House up close and personal.

"I'll need a copy of your driver's license and your social security numbers for clearance," she told me. "This will take a few weeks. A few months after the inauguration, we should be able to have a private tour. Mike, my fiancé, will let us know when everything has been okayed. You'll probably get only a day or two notice."

Tracy and I were excited at the possibility of a private tour of the executive mansion, but we tried not to have unrealistic expectations in case the arrangements fell through. One Friday evening we had several of our new friends from church over for an early dinner. One of the couples, Freda and Rudy, had "adopted" Kolby as their surrogate grandson. Because of our modest living associated with more medical training, entertaining friends had become a significant and infrequent event.

 I arrived home from work in time to assist with dinner. Tracy prepared a dish of angel hair pasta with squash, zucchini, snow peas, tomatoes, chicken, garlic and parmesan cheese. This culinary treat was saved for special occasions. I bought some fruit for a salad and mixed up a tart orange dressing to pour over it.

As I finished, the first couple arrived. I showed them into the living-family room. I heard a firm knock at the door. Kolby was a toddler, and the two of us answered the door. There stood Freda and Rudy.

Rudy wore a big grin. His arm was stuck straight out, perpendicular from his body, and clutched in his hand was a red string that hung to the porch floor.

"I got this for Kolby," Rudy said, not realizing something was missing.

I studied the limp string he held lightly in his hand. "What is it?" I asked after a second of silence.

"A Tweety Bird balloon," Rudy looked over his shoulder.

It dawned on each of us at the same moment. I picked up Kolby, and we stepped outside and looked into the sky. About fifty yards in the air, drifting off to the east, floated a big Tweety Bird balloon. It had broken off its string, and Tweety Bird had escaped to the freedom of the clear blue sky.

"See what Mr. and Mrs. Vacek got you!" I said to Kolby, and pointed to the sky. We all watched for a moment as Tweety drifted out of sight.

"Well, here's the string anyway." Rudy handed the red string to Kolby.

Kolby found as much fun with that string as he had with the box that contained his Christmas gift at Christmastime.

Tracy invited us to sit down in the family room for ten minutes before dinner would be served. Six adults settled into the room, and Kolby entertained us with his string. Allie had greeted our guests by sniffing and licking them. She was now in my chair, snuggled against my leg.

We sat around and engaged in small-talk for a few moments. All of a sudden I caught a whiff of one of a repugnant odor. Allie had tooted. I glanced around the room at our guests. Freda sat on my right and was the first to become visibly aware. Her lips curled, and she awk- wardly glanced my way. A split second later, the McDonalds, to my left, noticed the foul odor.

Kolby said, "What's that smell?"

Rudy was talking and didn't seem fazed by the putrid odor that filled the room. At the very instant when I opened my mouth to offer an explanation, Allie exaggeratingly stood up, looked at me, sniffed a couple of times, then hopped to the floor. She looked back at me, sniffed again, then trotted into the bedroom.

"Sorry for that smell, but that's our Allie. She is an odoriferous dog." In our family, we had grown accustomed to her flatulence.

"Oh, you're blaming that smell on the dog," Freda said with a smile.

I stammered while trying to offer an explanation.

Tracy rescued me. "It's time to eat."

We all took our assigned seats around the table, then Tracy filled our plates with pasta. I passed the garlic bread and the fruit salad around the table. Next I passed the orange sauce for the fruit salad.

Rudy caught Tracy's glance. Before she could stop him, he had poured a generous spoonful of tart orange sauce on his pasta.

Should I tell him? I wondered. No, I don't want to embarrass him. But it will ruin his meal. I looked around. Had anyone else noticed? No, everyone seemed preoccupied with their own dish. I decided to leave well enough alone and keep my mouth shut.

Tracy and I silently watched Rudy's every move until he took that first bite. He placed a large helping of pasta, dripping with lip-puckering citrus sauce into his mouth. For a moment he looked startled, then he said, "Oh, boy, that's wonderful. This pasta is delicious, and the sauce is most unusual and tasty."

I believe Freda was the only other person at the table who knew that orange sauce was designed for the fruit salad rather than the pasta, but none of us said a word. Rudy showered us with compliments on our wonderful Italian meal.

For the remainder of our time in Washington, every time we saw Rudy, he asked us for the recipe for that wonderful dish. We downplayed this as a secret family recipe. Still, every time we have pasta, I wonder if fruity tart sauce might top off the entrée and make it an "iron chef" meal.

The next Friday, Delaina informed me that our White House tour had been approved, and that it was scheduled for the following Sunday at one P.M. She gave us some strict rules and detailed instructions.

We arrived at the front of the White House in the visitors' lot one hour early. Around 12:45 Delaina arrived. She escorted us to the east gate, where we met her fiancé, Mike. He was on his bicycle and was in official Secret Service attire, an enforcement officer's uniform with a cyclist helmet and dark sunglasses.

We went through the security check, and then Tracy, Kolby, and I were escorted into the White House Press Room.

"Your guide will be with you in a moment," Mike said. "I'm on duty and will be patrolling the grounds. Here and the old Executive Office Building are the only places where picture taking is allowed."

The press room was smaller in reality than it appeared on television. We snapped a photograph of each of us behind the podium with the White House press room seal in the background.

In time, another Secret Service agent arrived and introduced himself as our tour guide. He escorted us to the front door of the White House, where the dignitaries are dropped off on their arrival. We walked through the Rose Garden, saw the room where VIPs are introduced to the staff, and toured the White House kitchen, where we even met one of the chefs.

"Just a minute," he said. "I've got something for you." The chef gave Kolby two boxes of M & M's stamped with the presidential seal.

We also got to see the Oval Office. During each part of the tour, the Secret Service agent offered tidbits of information. From the Oval Office, we walked to the Rose Garden. After seeing all of the White House except the residential quarters, we toured the old Executive Office Building across the street. The entire tour took a little more than an hour. It was one of those amazing, once-in-a-lifetime events.

After the tour, Mike reappeared. "How was it?" he asked.

"Amazing!" We thanked him for arranging an opportunity to do something few people get to do.

President George W. Bush had been in office for only five months. "The President will be returning from Camp David this afternoon around four. Would you like to see the helicopter, Marine One, land on the south lawn? And would you like to see the president? It's a long shot, but you might get to meet him and shake his hand."

"I don't know if we have the time," I joked, then said, "Would we? Are you kidding?"

"You'll have to leave and come back at three thirty."

We left through the same east gate through which we had arrived and strolled around the surrounding buildings until three thirty, then promptly returned. Our pass got us through the security check. We were escorted to the south lawn, where two rows of people were standing in parallel lines. To the left were little league ballplayers and their families. To the right were a couple hundred citizens of all types.

We were directed to the right, to stand behind a rope line on a two-lane asphalt running track that went around the perimeter of the south lawn.

At four P.M., a sound filled the air. The trees rustled. The wind blew. Suddenly three helicopters appeared. One headed toward the south lawn, and the other two veered away. I had read that three helicopters always arrived together, with one transporting the president. This was for national security purposes, so an enemy would not know which helicopter held the president.

The helicopter landed, and the propellers were turned off. A marine pushed a mobile staircase up to the door. Another marine opened the door, and then President Bush exited the plane. Patriotism welled up from deep within my soul, sending goose bumps up and down my spine. The crowd cheered.

Following President Bush were two dogs, Barney and Spot. Spot was famous as the offspring of Millie, George H. and Barbara Bush's dog. Spot was a Springer Spaniel. Born at the White House, she was the only dog to live in the executive mansion during two administrations. Barney was a black Scottish Terrier. I couldn't help wonder what Allie would do upon meeting these special canines.

Without hesitation, President Bush headed directly to the left where the lucky Little League ballplayers stood. A staff person brought both dogs to the right-hand line. This was our big chance to meet a president of the United States, and instead we met the "first dogs."

Kolby, Tracy and I petted Spot and Barney for several minutes, then the president and his dogs met in the middle and entered the back door of the White House. This event made our year in Washington, and our fifty-some weekend trips to the many memorials and national sites, complete.

We drove home in awed silence. Kolby was worn out and slept all the way. Back home Allie was excited to greet us. She stopped dead in her tracks and sniffed the three of us. She could smell the two dogs. She went from person to person studying the different smells. I had not seen her behave so inquisitively in the past. Her manner suggested she knew instinctively that these were two pretty important dogs.

But then in more typical fashion, she tossed her head and went on her way, as if to say, "Yeah, they may be national treasures, but I'm the true nobility around here."

CHAPTER 25

Living Down to the Last Moment

In August 2001, I completed my fellowship in interventional radiology in Washington. I had spent twenty-eight years of my life in some form of schooling. The time had come for me have a full-fledged career.

I accepted a radiology position in Topeka, Kansas, at a large radiology group practice of twenty-seven physicians. Tracy's dad had died from an aortic aneurysm rupture in November of 2000, and Tracy was happy to be only a five-hour drive from her mom.

Within weeks, Allie had introduced us to everyone in the neighborhood. On warm nights, we walked Allie around the cul-de-sac, and our neighbors stopped to pet her. She enjoyed these walks now as much as ever, even though she was nearly eleven.

Our next-door neighbors were the Andersons. Deb Anderson was a veterinarian. Allie and Dr. Anderson hit it off instantly. "We've found our new vet," I said to Tracy during one of our first walks around the neighborhood.

The move to Topeka proved to be one of the easiest ones we had ever undertaken. Each of our family traditions carried over to our new home. We had our Easter egg hunts and tossed hard-boiled eggs to Allie as she pranced across our large fenced-in backyard. She chased the rabbits around the yard, nearly catching them. She was as excited about Halloween and Christmas as she had ever been.

One weekend Tracy's mom and brother Shawn came for a visit. This particular trip was a bit different from the others as Alice was bringing Pippin for the first time. While Allie and Pippin had spent a lot of time playing at Tracy's folks' home, Allie always teased and irritated Pippin.

Pippin was high-strung, and Tracy's mom had picked up a couple of tranquilizers from her veterinarian to calm Pippin for the trip. When they pulled into our driveway late in the afternoon, Pippin had that glazed, far-off look of sedation in her eyes.

Allie was in the house when I led Pippin into the backyard, closed the gate and let her loose. Soon Tracy opened the back door, and before anyone realized it, Allie, at around sixteen pounds, came barking and growling at Pippin, who weighed in at around ninety-five pounds. For the first time, Pippin was invading Allie's home turf. In typical alpha-dog style, Allie charged at Pippin, growling and barking, as if to say, "What are you doing at my house? Get out of my yard!"

In the past, Pippin had taken this as dog play. This time Pippin charged at Allie, teeth exposed. I grabbed Allie and scooped her into my arms, but Pippin continued to pursue her, and despite my best efforts, Pippin's teeth sank into Allie's flesh, biting her neck. In an instant, Allie's white fur was covered in blood.

Allie shrieked and squirmed to fight, all the more determined to tackle this superior fighting dog. I struggled mightily to fend off Pippin's charge, while holding Allie up in the air safely out of reach. The force with which Pippin lunged nearly knocked me down. I was angry with Pippin and afraid for Allie's life all at once. I refereed, Pippin charged and Allie fought back; we created quite a commotion!

Finally, Tracy came running and grabbed Allie from my arms while I tried to restrain Pippin. The effect of the drugs made her look as wild and ferocious as a rabid dog.

After calming Pippin, I raced in to see if Allie was okay. She had several cuts throughout her back and a larger laceration on her tail. Pippin's open mouth had been only millimeters from the vital structures of Allie's neck. Had Pippin penetrated Allie's cervical spine, I believe her neck would have snapped in two, like a small twig. The whole event shook everyone up.

I took Allie straight to Deb's, and she examined her thoroughly.

"Only a few cuts," she concluded.

"That's a relief. Is she up-to-date on her shots?"

"She is."

"Good." I was relieved.

When I brought Allie back into the house, she quivered, shivered and shook as if she'd been stranded in a snowstorm. But seeing Pippin outside with only a glass door between them, she perked up and displayed the same alpha-dog response toward Pippin as before. But Pippin just lay there. The energy she had expended traveling and fighting with Allie had worn her out. She was under the deep influence of the sedatives, and as docile as could be.

We were much more cautious with Allie and Pippin from that day forward. Except for cats, nothing else frightened Allie.

The years passed quickly. We had our yearly Christmas cards as a point of reference. On Kolby's first birthday, we had taken a picture of him with Allie. We used this picture as our Christmas card that year. This started a tradition we continued each year. Sometimes the picture included Allie and Kolby, and sometimes Tracy and I posed with both of them.

Our Christmas card photograph had room for at least one more child. Not too long after our move to Topeka, we began to discuss fertility testing.

Around 2004, when Allie was thirteen years old, I noticed changes in her. Her beautifully expressive dark eyes were clouding over. And her once-acute hearing had dulled.

We spoke to Dr. Anderson about Allie's eyes. She diagnosed the problem as most likely cataracts. The surgery to remove the diseased lenses would cost fifteen hundred dollars. Tracy and I saw this expenditure as necessary, as the surgery would improve Allie's quality of life.

Before the surgery was scheduled, Dr. Anderson suggested we have a consultation and get a second opinion from the specialist at Kansas State University School of Veterinary Medicine, in Manhattan, only fifty miles away.

After a thorough ophthalmologic examination, it was clear Allie had been misdiagnosed. She had macular degeneration; cataract surgery would be of no benefit. Faced with this disappointing news, we brought her home.

Even though there would be a gradual decline, the end result was complete loss of sight. It broke my heart to think of her groping around blindly in the dark. But I reminded myself that dogs have keen senses, and when one fails another takes over.

As Allie's eyesight gradually declined to complete blindness, I marveled at how well she adapted. She simply refused to let something like visual impairment prevent her from enjoying life. I appreciated this example and lesson more than all the others she had taught me. Make the most out of each difficulty you face in this life, never giving in to despair. I came to believe the adage, when life gives you lemons, make lemonade. Allie certainly did.

One evening shortly afterwards, Allie came to jump up on the bed as she had done several times a day for thirteen plus years. This time she missed and fell back to the floor. She hopped up immediately, then looked around the room as if to see if anyone was watching. I remained quiet. Instead of attempting to hop up again, she lay down at the foot of the bed. She wasn't hurt, but her pride seemed bruised.

I realized in that instant that Allie had entered her golden years.

It seemed that only yesterday she had been a puppy, full of exuberance and unlimited energy. The day-to-day changes were small and gradual. Allie had been growing older with each passing day, but we had not detected these changes until now. Over night, she suddenly looked old. This brought Tracy and me much sadness, realizing that the end could be just around the corner. A small, sick feeling developed in my gut. Over the next several years, on multiple occasions, this feeling would grow more intense.

Tracy and I found a dowry chest to place at the foot of our bed. Allie quickly learned to jump onto the chest and then onto the bed. As was usually the case, she was courageous and determined, not easily giving up.

But our growing concern about Allie was balanced by a joyous event. In August 2003, Tracy had delivered our second son, Weston McLinn. Allie accepted Weston unconditionally into her life. She had been protective of Kolby, always following him around as if trying to catch his fall, and we would find Allie lying in Weston's room at the foot of his crib.

Even though Allie's body had begun to age and she had grown more fragile, her disposition remained youthful and ornery. She was a youthful soul at heart.

One afternoon when I was at work, Tracy called me, "You'll never guess what your daughter did this time. Here she is, over fifteen years old, nearly blind and going deaf, and yet she managed to catch a bunny, bring it inside, and eat half of it for dinner."

A scene from a Bugs Bunny cartoon popped into my mind. I could see Allie with her prey in her mouth and her white fur bloodied while Elmer Fudd said, "I killed that wascally wabbit."

"I found Allie on the couch," Tracy continued, "eating her prey as if she were king of the jungle."

"She's acting like a puppy again."

The puppy-like behavior never completely left her, but there were more and more days between each instance. One afternoon on a weekend in late 2006, I heard a noise followed by a yelp. Allie had fallen down the stairs. After a brief exam, I determined she was okay. The more these things happened, the more my fears were affirmed: Her physical body was aging and wearing out. There was no escaping this natural progression.

I began praying that God would take Allie in her sleep. I didn't know if I could put her down or make the right decision at the right time. Would I be too selfish to let her go when it was time? Praying for her to die in her sleep peacefully provided some small comfort—not a lot, but some.

Tracy and I had been planning a family trip to Florida for both a vacation and a radiology conference. This would be our first trip away for an extended period—two weeks—without Allie. She was over sixteen. Her age alone caused us to hesitate regarding this trip, but the plans had been arranged for months and the boys were excited about the upcoming vacation. We reluctantly decided to carry on with our plans. We went to great lengths to hide our suitcases while we packed, as Allie knew an open suitcase filled with clothes meant we were going on a trip, herself included.

As the date of the trip approached, Tracy and I grew more worried about Allie. We asked a friend who had babysat for Kolby and Weston to stay at our home the two weeks we would be gone to doggy sit.

The day of departure finally arrived. Allie looked so dejected as we handed her off to Nancy and got into the car to leave on our trip! That look on her face tormented us. We called home and checked on her daily. Each report was upbeat and favorable. Allie seemed to be doing fine without us. These reports provided a modicum of comfort.

She had become the oldest dog ever in our family. She had surpassed Kupid's record age of fifteen and a half years. We had been feeding Allie Pupperonis from age one, and she had now reached sixteen-plus years. I began to refer to Pupperonis as the fountain of youth, even encouraging my folks to start eating them so they could live on and on like Allie.

We returned home from Florida the week before Labor Day 2008.

Allie was elated to see us. For about twenty-four hours all was right with the world once again. I returned to work, and we settled into our usual routine.

The next day I was at the hospital. Around ten A.M., Tracy called. "Something's wrong with Allie," she said, crying. "She can't stop throwing up."

That sick feeling in the pit of my stomach grew stronger. "How many times?"

"A lot. She's so very weak."

"You better get her up to Deb's."

Throughout the day I got several more calls from Tracy. The last call of the day was around four P.M., and it was from Dr. Anderson.

"How is she?" I asked cautiously.

"Well, I'm surprised her labs are as good as they are," the vet told me. "Her liver and kidney functions are a little elevated. She's very weak and dehydrated, and she's still throwing up, but much less frequently."

"Deb, let me ask you your honest opinion." I managed to choke the words out. "Is she suffering? Should we put her down?"

"I think you should give this a little time and see how she responds," Deb answered.

"Okay, but you'll be candid with us with, won't you?"

I arrived home in time to go to Deb's clinic at five thirty with Tracy. When we got there, Allie looked lethargic and gaunt, but still wagged her tail when she heard my voice.

"Boy, Deb, is she really hanging in there?"

"I think so," Deb said.

"What's next?" I asked.

"Well, she can have her IV for five days. We should know by then what we're dealing with, whether it's a flare-up of her Crohn's or a severe case of gastroenteritis. I'd like to keep her overnight."

Tracy began to cry.

"Deb, Allie's only spent one night of her life in a kennel. I can give the shots or anything else she needs, and we'll have her back here in the morning at whatever time you say." I began negotiating.

"I suppose that's okay," Deb said reluctantly. "I know this is hard, but we have to be extremely methodical about this. No food at all for her. None!" Deb's tone was firm but compassionate.

The next several days were extremely difficult as we stuck to this schedule. Tracy and I, and even the boys, were haunted by the realization that Allie's life might be coming to an end. Every afternoon Tracy went to the animal hospital and spent two to three hours with Allie. She would crawl into Allie's cage and lie next to her. Sometimes she would cry. At other times, she would talk to Allie and reassure her that if it was her time, or if she was tired, she could let go. After bringing Allie home at the end of the day, I injected the medications and administered them on a four-hour schedule throughout the night so she could spend the night at home with us.

Then something short of miraculous occurred. When Tracy went in to see Allie the fifth afternoon of her hospital stay, Allie was standing in her cage, sporting a happy expression as if to say, "Okay, enough of this. I'm ready to be discharged and get on with my life, whatever time I have left!"

It was a great day in our house when our beloved Chelsea Alexis came home to stay. We didn't know when the end would come. We didn't even want to think about it. All we knew was that we weren't ready to let go, and fortunately for us, neither was Allie.

We spent the next days and months cherishing every moment we had with her. If she had been spoiled before, she was now the queen of Sheba. Tracy had promised her one afternoon while she lay in her cage at the hospital that she could eat turkey for the rest of her life if she pulled through. To Allie's final hour, she enjoyed turkey at least one meal a day.

Of course, I knew that Allie's final chapter had begun. She would not be on this earth much longer. But I also understood how important it was to make the most of every day we had with her.

I think Allie somehow knew that we would need another ten months to come to grips with the inevitable. Like so many times before, Allie was teaching us one of life's important lessons: to live each day to the fullest and to enjoy the comfort of our loved ones every moment. This lesson I took to heart.

CHAPTER 26

The Long Good-Bye

Even though Allie's eyes had dulled, we had been able to see the glow that told us she loved life and loved us too much to give up. But lately that glow had become an empty gaze. Her wonderfully dark, expressive, human-like eyes had lost their brilliance.

In the midst of overwhelming emotions, desperation and reflection on the past seventeen years, I realized the greatest act of love and kindness that we could do for Allie was to let her go.

Allie had given us her unconditional love, her unwavering loyalty and a lifetime full of cherished memories. Now, it was time to say good-bye.

On Friday, March 6, 2009, Tracy took Allie to the vet for a checkup. We had noticed a few more discolored moles and growths on her back and became concerned. During this visit, Tracy spoke candidly with Dr. Anderson and asked her pointed, tough, end-of-life questions.

"How will we know if we're hanging on too long or if we have forgotten Allie's best interests?"

"How is she acting?" Dr. Anderson asked. "Has she lost her appe-tite? Is she often confused? Does she get stuck in a room or in a corner and is unable to get out? If not, then she probably isn't suffering."

That evening Tracy and I discussed the consultation. I was all too familiar with the symptoms Dr. Anderson had mentioned as they were also generally present in dementia or various forms of Alzheimer's in humans. Fortunately, we could answer each question with absolute certainty: No! I tucked Dr. Anderson's words of wisdom and caution into the deeper recesses of my mind.

The weekend was no different than any other in recent months. Allie spent much of her day sleeping in the closet on a pile of dirty clothes. Her internal alarm clock rang on schedule, and we fed her at eight A.M. She went outside and pottied, then we took her upstairs. She slept until eleven. When awakened she gently whined, reminding us that it was time for her turkey treat.

She spent the noon hour hoping for a morsel of food to drop from our plates. From one until four thirty, she slept in the closet again.

Tracy home-schooled both boys. Being a teacher, she had them on a strict and regimented schedule. During the day, between lessons, Tracy could check on Allie frequently. Allie spent some of her afternoon sleeping on a blanket in the corner of the school room. Having Allie close-by was a constant source of comfort for Tracy.

On Wednesdays I worked from home. Allie had endearingly cho-sen to spend every Wednesday with me while I worked, my special time with her each week. This was time I had come to cherish. Now Allie spent the afternoon sleeping on the couch next to my computer workstation. She had a special blanket with a picture of a Bichon on it. Frequently during the afternoon, I would take a couple of minutes and sit next to Allie on the couch and scratch her ears. She had always enjoyed this attention. She would stretch, roll onto her side and express her satisfaction with a heavy sigh. However, lately, she barely responded to my touch.

Recently, it appeared Allie's days began to blend together. After her morning meal and a trip outside, she slept until noon. She might have slept right through the noon hour, but we were vigilant and aroused her for a noon snack. After a second trip outside, she spent the remainder of the day in the closet sleeping. After an evening meal she slept until bedtime. We awakened her and took her outside to do her business one final time before retiring for a good night's sleep. For the past several days, I noticed her engaging spirit had grown weak and lethargic. Every simple activity became difficult and cumbersome.

Saturday and Sunday, the schedule stayed nearly the same. Even Monday was fairly standard. On Tuesday, before going to work, I checked on Allie. She barely aroused as I studied her.

"I'm worried about Allie," I said to Tracy as I kissed her good-bye.

"Why? What's different?" Tracy responded sleepily.

"I don't know. She appears despondent." I hadn't used that term for years, and the only times I had used this common word, which also had a hidden medical meaning, was when death was imminent or dementia had progressed to near incoherence.

"Okay, I'll keep an eye on her," Tracy said.

Around ten thirty the next morning, Tracy called me at work. Her voice was hoarse, and it held the distinct tone I knew so well. She had been crying.

"She doesn't seem to recognize me."

"Is she eating?"

"Yes."

"Does she act like she's in pain?"

"Not really."

"Anything else?"

"Yes, she let me hold her the whole time Kolby was doing his reading, and you know that's not Allie."

"True," I said. "Well, let's wait and see what happens."

After a palpable pause, Tracy said, "Okay, I'll let you know," then hung up.

I sat at work in silence, trying to keep my composure. Memories flooded my mind. Silent images passed through the crevices of my brain in slow motion. "Just get through the day," I whispered quietly.

I had a meeting outside the office scheduled for two o'clock, but I stopped by the house first. Tracy was right. Allie sat on her lap in the school room while Tracy worked with Kolby. Allie had always been so independent, almost to a fault. She would never have let us hold her for a long period of time. She would have licked us on the cheek, then squirmed emphatically, as if to say, "There, you know I like you. Now you can put me down."

But there she lay, despondent, on Tracy's lap. There it was again—that word of frailty and impending doom.

"You're right," I said. "Something has changed. Do you want to take her to the vet?"

"No." Tracy was stern. "We were just there Friday. Let's see how she does tonight."

I drove off to my meeting, a migraine headache building.

The hours passed, and my headache worsened. That evening when I came home, I took my suitcase from the closet. I was to be out in central Kansas to perform a medical procedure on Wednesday and was supposed to leave that night.

"Can't you stay?" Kolby asked.

"I'm sorry, son, I have to go. I missed going the last few weeks."

I pulled out of the driveway. Allie remained in Tracy's arms, and the four of them stood at the front door waving good-bye. I had a two-and-a-half-hour drive ahead of me. My brain was pounding, and my thoughts were consumed with Allie.

"Is this it?" I kept repeating to myself. "Is this the beginning of the end?"

Thirty minutes later, I called home. "I'm coming back home. Will you talk to Mr. Waters, the hospital C.E.O., and let him know I won't be coming out to central Kansas this week?"

"Okay."

I called my sister Kim from Salina. She had been an important part of Allie's life, and I felt she should be notified of Allie's worsening condition.

After a half hour, I pulled into the driveway. Tracy told me Kim and her Poodle, Sassy, were on their way.

It was a long night, suffering with a migraine, worrying about Allie, and trying to sleep. As for Tracy, she was up with Allie most of the night.

By morning of Wednesday, March 11, not much had changed. Neither Allie nor I was better. Allie wandered around the bedroom like she was lost or had misplaced something. To see her like that was a crushing blow. She had always been so sharp and so alert. Even when her hearing and eyesight failed, her sense of smell had taken over, and she appeared not to miss a beat.

"I called Dr. Anderson," Tracy told me. "Kim and I will take her to the vet this morning."

"Good." I was pleased we were seeking expert advice.

About an hour later the three returned. "What did she say?" I asked.

"Deb's concerned that Allie may have had a stroke. She agrees she's much different today than last Friday. She gave her a shot of steroids."

"Did she have any suggestions?"

"Yes, she wants to see her Friday, to see if there's any improvement. There's about a twenty-percent chance she'll get better."

"That's all?" I asked slowly. "And if the shot doesn't help?"

Tracy began to sob. "We'll have to think about putting her down."

I sat in silence, Allie beside me on the bed, with the sounds of Tracy's muffled sobs in the background.

Soon after, I thought I detected a little improvement in Allie. Was I thinking clearly, I wondered, or was it wishful thinking?

Later in the day, Tracy voiced what I was thinking. "I believe she's a little better."

We tried desperately to reassure each other. "Better? In what way?" I asked.

"Well, she wagged her tail. She hasn't done that for several days."

I could tell Tracy was grasping at straws. "That's a good sign." I said unconvincingly.

"And I noticed her appetite has improved."

She clung to faint hope. "And she's even a little more alert," I, too, persisted with the charade, and our false hope got us through the rest of the day.

My migraine (not surprisingly) was a whopper and had already lasted twenty-four hours with no relief in sight. Allie and I lay side-by-side in the bed, convalescing. I knew my headache would ultimately go away, and I would get better. But would Allie? I feared the answer.

For the second straight night, Tracy spent much of the time awake with Allie. Around one thirty in the morning, I woke up suddenly. Tracy was coming out of the closet with Allie in her arms and tears streaming down her face.

"It's time," she said.

CHAPTER 27

Letting Go

The remainder of the night passed by slowly. I counted the seconds, minutes and hours until the sun appeared over the horizon, then got up to face the day. Allie and Tracy lay next to each other on the bed, resting peacefully, if for only a moment. I got ready for work, then glanced at the two of them on the bed, a scene I have been able to picture in my mind nearly every day for the past seventeen and a half years. I let them sleep and headed to the hospital.

It was Thursday, March 12, 2009. Tracy made arrangements for Dr. Anderson to come to our home around eight thirty the next morning. My colleagues agreed to cover for me on Friday.

The previous night, I had been clinging to the desperate hope that somehow Allie would die in her sleep before morning. I had helped my dad euthanize many pets and even more strays. I was horrified at having to do this to our special little Allie.

Tracy told the boys. Kolby's reaction was heartbreaking. "Why do kids have to go through so much pain?" he asked me.

"I don't know, Kolby."

"I wish I had never been born," he said.

"I know it's painful, but if you hadn't been born, how would you have known Allie and how could she have known you?"

Kolby was sad and very quiet as Tracy explained to him and Weston what was going to happen when Dr. Anderson arrived. They had spent the evening drawing and painting a good-bye picture for Allie. The picture Kolby painted was filled with exceptional detail. He had painted a very realistic picture of Allie and at the top painted in big red letters, "In loving memory of our Allie."

The sight of it was very touching, and the perpetual lump in my throat grew larger as I soaked in this overwhelming act of love.

The evening was awful. I found myself wavering between holding it together and falling apart. Our hearts were breaking. This little, gentle animal, who had done nothing harmful to anyone, was suffering.

I thought of death row and what it must be like to know the hour of death was set. All that was left was to wait while the seconds, minutes, and hours ticked slowly by. We tried to maintain the routine as much as possible, and we gave Allie the special foods she could eat. She enjoyed hard-boiled eggs and turkey, and all the Pupperoni treats she wanted.

Both Kolby and Weston cried themselves to sleep. Around eleven thirty P.M., we lay down on the bed, Allie between us, as she had always been for seventeen years. I silently prayed for inner strength for each one of us to get through this. I prayed for Allie not to experience any physical pain, and I prayed for one last time that God would allow her to pass away in her sleep. But if not, could she have a peaceful night? Then all three of us fell asleep.

At one thirty A.M., Allie sat straight up in bed. I woke immediately, and I carried her into the closet. In a few moments, she lay on the floor, trying to get to sleep. She appeared more peaceful than she had the previous few nights.

"Thank you, God," I whispered, and then lay down, my head against hers. I recalled all the wonderful memories. I knew I'd now have to rely on memories for any comfort as it was only seven hours before Allie would be just that—a precious memory.

For the next several hours in the quiet darkness of the morning, while I lay stroking the fur of her frail, aged body, an entire lifetime passed before my eyes.

I knew that Tracy, the boys, and I were about to perform the greatest act of kindness that a man can show his pet. I also knew it would be the most difficult task I had yet completed.

That morning, Friday, March 13, 2009, time stood still. Kim was staying at my parents' home, and she and Sassy arrived around seven thirty. Mom arrived around seven forty-five with her Poodle, Sugar Bear.

Weston, who was five, was very inquisitive. "Allie's going to die today, Aunt Kim," he said matter-of-factly. This was the first time I had heard those words spoken out loud. It shook my inner core.

We fed Allie multiple times. She got her usual breakfast. I gave her some turkey. Tracy gave her a hard-boiled egg. I gave her a Pupperoni.

We watched the time continually. During some eerie moments of silence, I swore I could hear the seconds ticking off the clock. At around eight fifteen, we gave Allie another helping of turkey.

Tracy took Allie outside one final time. It was something so ordinary and so much a part of every day, yet it was clear that it would be the last time Allie would pass through the door of her home, set foot on her lawn, and sniff the air. Each final act was gut wrenching.

"Why do you have to think like that?" I silently reprimanded myself, as if that would somehow help things. That was the point, if there was any point at all. Nothing could make this any easier. This was the natural order of things. That was my only comfort. If God designed such a wonderful little creature as Allie, He must have some purpose for her in the afterlife, I reassured myself.

At eight thirty Kolby and I stood at the front door, gazing out into the slightly overcast, cool morning. Dr. Anderson was uncharacteristically late. We stood leaning against each other, staring out the door. Around eight forty Dr. Anderson and her vet assistant, Carla, pulled up.

"This is it," I thought.

The next minutes passed in a daze. We had Allie's special blanket. We had a scissors ready to cut off a few locks of Allie's hair, a small remembrance for Tracy, our sons and me.

Tracy sat on the couch, and I spread Allie's blanket across Tracy's lap. Then we each took a moment to hug and hold Allie and to say good-bye in our own way. I placed Allie on the blanket. Tears streamed down Tracy's face and mine.

Sugar Bear and Sassy sat in unusual silence. Allie truly had been the matriarchal pet of the family—a role she had held for ten years, since she was seven. Allie had seen many of the family pets come and go, while she just kept on going—another unique example of just how special she was.

Dr. Anderson explained her every move. Weston remained the most curious of us all. He hadn't grasped the finality of it. Not yet, anyway.

Dr. Anderson injected the anesthetic. Allie yelped and whimpered. In fewer than five minutes, Allie's body went limp. The anesthetic had taken its effect. Dr. Anderson could now insert the needle into Allie's vein in her front leg without causing our beloved pet any discomfort whatsoever.

In a matter of seconds, she had successfully accessed the vein, and the push of her thumb on the plunger of the syringe injected the lethal medicine into Allie's veins. We remained by her side when she breathed her last breath.

Allie was gone. At 8:53 A.M. on Friday, March 13, 2009, the final second of her cherished life was over. She lay in the comfort of her most familiar place, Tracy's arms.

Tracy choked out her final request of Allie. "Be sure and look for me when my life is over."

Allie died peacefully in our home surrounded by the most important people in her life, her family: Mom, who had picked her out of the litter; Kim, who was Allie's first surrogate master until she was given to Tracy; myself, Allie's secondary master; Kolby, Allie's first little brother;

Weston, Allie's second little brother; and of course, Tracy, Allie's loving master, on whom Allie had showered unconditional love and continual devotion.

After a couple of minutes, we cut a few more locks of hair from Allie's ears and then wrapped her gently in her blanket. Deb and Carla gathered up their medical supplies and instruments, then Tracy handed Allie's body over to Dr. Anderson. It was final.

I couldn't believe it. I didn't want to believe it. I had wished it a dream, but the gnawing pain tugging on my heartstrings reminded me it was all too real.

Weston now understood that Allie was gone. He began to sob, while Dr. Anderson carried Allie's body out of our home and placed her in the car. Allie would be cremated later that day.

To store Allie's ashes, Tracy had picked out a beautiful wooden box with a small ceramic figure of a Bichon on top. That box of Allie's cremated remains was some day to be placed in Tracy's casket.

A couple of hours after Allie died, Kolby wrote a poem for her. Though he was only ten at the time, his way with words was well beyond his years.

I will tell a story about a great pet,

Who changed the lives of many,

And who to us was meant

She might have looked like a regular dog,

But, through our perspective that was entirely wrong.

Not because she could do tricks,

Not because she was naughty,

Although she could do all those things,

Forgive me for being a little haughty.

I will begin a long time ago,

When she was put in a box,

For someone who would love her so,

She was a present for my mother.

When she came out of the box that Christmas day,

She was a present for my mother

While Father was away.

So through the years when my brother and I were born,

She welcomed us warmly to our home,

I can't explain how much she loved us,

Even in great mourn.

And when seventeen years have passed,

I wish it never came,

The everlasting sleep

Until we meet again.

So, I must finish this poem,

But, I know I will see her again,

In that great city of Gold.

The End.

We knew that one day we would have another pet to occupy the space in our home and our hearts. We knew that pet would be special and unique in its own way. But at that moment, I could not imagine that any dog—no matter how wonderful and special it was, or how special it would become to each of us—could ever replace Allie.

She was one of a kind with whom we proudly shared our house, our hearts and our lives. She stole our hearts and occupied that special place deep in our soul, reserved for unforgettable, cherished memories.

Her name had been Chelsea Alexis. She would remain, "Always Allie"!

Epilogue

The days and weeks passed by slowly. After two months, Tracy asked if there was something wrong with her. Would she ever get over the loss of Allie? I tried to be consoling, but I had asked this very question of myself.

After six months we began to consider bringing another puppy in our lives. Finally, Tracy contacted my mom and asked her to pick out our second Bichon Frise.

After some searching, Mom and Tracy located a Bichon breeder in Springfield, Missouri. Mom, Tracy and the boys headed south in late August 2009, and they met our next furry, four-legged daughter. As expected, Mom picked out just the right puppy for our home.

We named our new puppy Allie Adele and decided to call her "Addie."

That's how it was the first time I laid eyes upon Addie. I knew she was that special dog who would steal our hearts and fill us with a lifetime of love and memories that we would cherish all our days.

TIDBITS AND TREATS

Pets don't come with an owner's manual. More often than not, and especially with Allie, it is the pet who teaches us. Still, there are things to know, and information to be had, that can be helpful to pet owners and caregivers. The following tips, strategies, and problem-solving techniques relate to specific chapters of the book. For additional resources, or to connect with Dr. Van Camp directly in relation to speaking engagements, promotional or educational opportunities, visit www.alwaysallie.com. Also, be sure to sign up for our online contests at www.alwaysallie.com.

Chapter 1
Choose the Right Breed

On average, a couple will have five dogs throughout their married lives. Locating the best breed and the right companion for you and your family can be an overwhelming task. Check out Mom's Corner on our website, www.alwaysallie.com, for tips and suggestions regarding how to select the perfect canine for your family's needs. See our checklist and interactive pet selection tool at www.alwaysallie.com and keep a look out for our occasional promotional giveaways.

Chapter 2
Get Fit With Fido

People benefit from routines, too. This tidbit is for the owner. The American Heart Association recommends thirty minutes of exercise five days a week. Why not make ten or fifteen of those thirty minutes of exercise time walking your dog. Several important things will happen when you include your dog in your exercise program. First, you will become more consistent with doing exercise, as Fido will not let you miss a day of walking. Once this becomes part of his schedule, you'll find it mighty difficult to skip a session. Second, you will spend more quality time bonding with your dog. Finally, you'll be in better physical condition. And so will your dog.

Chapter 3
Training and Feeding

There are many things to consider and to remember when it comes to training your new puppy. Selecting the best puppy school is paramount. On our website we have given our advice and relayed techniques suggested by some of the leading animal behavior specialists and authorities. You can review these guidelines and suggestions at www.alwaysallie.com.

Another extremely important decision you will make that will affect your puppy for its entire life is selecting the best dog food to meet its specific nutritional and dietary needs. We discuss the various requirements at each different stage of development on our website. Sign up for our free electronic newsletter at www.alwaysallie.com.

Chapter 4
What Would Your Dog Do?

Here's a tidbit for "type A personality" owners. Perhaps you find that you are overreactive to irritations in your life. Have you ever found yourself responding negatively to something that is frustrating, rather than remaining calm, cool and collected? Maybe you are run down and worn out, or have fallen into a negative habit of reacting before stopping and thinking about a better way to handle a difficult situation. Try this: Apply some of the techniques you have used with obedience training with your pet to your own personal life. When training your pet, the behavior authorities suggest calm mannerisms, firm but compassionate commands, consistent, deliberate and methodical actions. Next time you encounter a difficult situation in your life, try thinking about following these same principles: remain calm, stand your ground with compassion and understanding, be consistent with each difficulty, think through how you want to handle the particular situation, and be deliberate in your actions and methodical in your response.

Chapter 5
Create a Safe Haven

Is your dog an indoor or an outdoor pet? Whether inside or out, having a safe and secure yard or kennel is of great importance. There are multiple ways to keep your dog safe in your yard. A smaller fenced-in area within the larger yard or an electronic boundary are a couple of ways to escape-proof your property.

What if your dog does manage to leave the confines of your safe haven? How do you conduct a successful pet search? What about pet trackers and pet finders? What do these organizations offer? An implanted identification chip is an invaluable way to ensure that your dog can be identified if she happens to wander off. Each of these topics and many others regarding your dog's security are described in detail on our website. You can review our suggestions and check out our recommended links at www.alwaysallie.com. Be sure and participate in our online contests and our occasional promotional giveaways at www.alwaysallie.com.

Chapter 6

Going Places With Your Dog

Should your dog be kenneled when you travel? This remains a controversial topic. You can see our thoughts on this subject at www.alwaysallie.com. What about traveling with your pet? How or what can you do to assist your dog with car travel? Is air travel for your pet an acceptable mode of transport? What about pet accommodations on the road? How do you locate pet-friendly hotels? Have you heard of pet travel agencies? These agencies assist with boarding accommodations during your trip. See our suggestions at www.alwaysallie.com.

Chapter 7

Moving? Plan Ahead

Allie was extremely adaptable, but not all dogs are this unflappable. There are some techniques you can use to make an insecure dog feel more secure when a move is inevitable. We have listed several tried-and-true techniques under "dealing with that impending move" on our website, www.alwaysallie.com.

Chapter 8
Have a Healthy Dog

What about your pet's medical care? How do you select the right veterinarian? When does your pet need her vaccinations? What are the pet licensing laws and requirements for your state? What about specific breeds, are there any unique traits you should know? How do you evaluate your pet's eyesight or hearing changes? What about catastrophic illness? Is there insurance for your pet? We have provided a set of general pet care recommendations. We address whether or not pet insurance is right for you and how to purchase insurance. We answer questions about pet health, including vaccination and healthy check-up schedules. Check out these suggestions and our recommended links at www.alwaysallie.com. And remember to sign up for our occasional online contests and promotional giveaways.

Chapter 9
Monitoring Health Conditions

Just as you would for a person with a chronic illness like diabetes or inflammatory bowel disease, if your pet suffers from a chronic disease, you must educate yourself as the primary caregiver. We have provided some links to chronic conditions that are common to dogs. We have also described some of the more frequent problems associated with various breeds. Does your dog suffer from a debilitating illness? Share your story with us at www.alwaysallie.com. You can also check out some of our recommendations regarding long-term care for chronic ailments on our website.

Chapter 10
What's Your Pedigree?

Here's a tidbit for the owner. Do you know where you come from? Have you ever spent any time looking up or studying about your ancestors? With technology today, it's much easier to take a glimpse at your heritage—your human pedigree. There are several places to look for your genealogy. One of the best websites is www.ancestry.com. Knowing Allie's heritage offered insight into why she behaved some of the ways she did. She loved to root in the dirt. After studying her background, we found that she was bred as a hunting dog, specifically for small rodents. We also learned that she was bred for nobility, offering an explanation for her unwavering confidence. These two details about her genetics gave explanations for some of her behaviors. Perhaps, knowing your ancestors will be insightful, too.

🐾

Chapter 11
Post-op Care

Like people, most dogs will have at least one major surgery throughout their life. Knowing how to care for your pet post-operatively is important. How long will recovery take? What is the expected outcome or prognosis? These are just a few of the questions for which we provide answers at www.alwaysallie.com. Be on the lookout for our promotional giveaways at www.alwaysallie.com.

Chapter 12
Did Fido Just Shun Me?

Some time during your pet's life he will likely give you "the cold shoulder" or "silent treatment." It's comical in some respects, but also exposes your four-legged child's sensitive side. Time,

patience and understanding make this brief period of difficulty more bearable for your pet and for you. Share your experiences regarding the recipient of the frustrated pet's wrath at
www.alwaysallie.com. See also our many thoughts and suggestions for how to deal with this issue if and when it occurs.

Chapter 13
"My Dog Just 'Knows'"

Dogs are highly aware of their surroundings and acutely in tune
with our moods. They know immediately when our demeanor
has changed. They pick up on our emotional state sometimes
quicker than our mate, family, or friends. This quality makes
them unique. Allie knew when Tracy and I were hurting and
often provided us comfort. Tell us how your pet comforted
you in your hour of need at www.alwaysallie.com. Sign up
and participate in our online contests for gifts and awards at
www.alwaysallie.com.

Chapter 14
Give in to Love

Growing up, my dad often kept a distance from our pets. I'm
certain there were some obvious explanations for this. He was a
veterinarian, so he needed to be able to remain objective when
treating our furry, family members. Like any good doctor, he
wanted to prevent his personal feelings from clouding his best
judgment when it came to challenging medical decisions. Many
people, for various reasons, try to maintain a distance from
their pet, always attempting to keep them in their place and
often trying to maintain a realistic perspective. Have you ever
heard anyone say, "They're just pets." Although I can understand this sentiment, I believe these folks are missing one of

the most important aspects of being a pet owner. Pets love their families unconditionally. They are happy to give you their loyalty and their affection. Don't be afraid or hesitant to do the same. Letting your guard down and accepting and embracing these deep feelings is in and of itself healthy for all our relationships, both human and animal. It is when we are willing and courageous enough to be vulnerable that we really begin to comprehend love. And it's through these experiences that we truly live life to its fullest.

Chapter 15
Dogs Like Gifts, Too

On special occasions, go ahead a make a fuss over your pet. You'll develop an even stronger bond with man's best friend.

You might be surprised at how much pets love the holidays. They sense the excitement and thrill of the season much like children. Now that Allie is gone, I feel her absence all the more from Thanksgiving until New Year's Day. Her excitement was infectious and warmed my heart every Christmas. See some of our ideas for how to make the holiday special at www.alwaysallie.com. Tell us your story about the holidays with your four-legged child. Also, be sure to look for our online contests and promotional giveaways at www.alwaysallie.com.

Chapter 16
Preparing for a Move

Even though some dogs, like Allie, appear overly adaptable, always be prepared that a move might be difficult. There are numerous variables to consider: age of your dog, how long you have lived at the location you are leaving, the reason for your move, and any other impending changes due to divorce or death. These factors can have a great influence on how your pet handles the move. Check out www.alwaysallie.com to find ways to make your move more palatable for your pooch.

Chapter 17

Doggie, Meet Baby

Each pet is different when it comes to children. Don't underestimate the effect that jealousy can have on a dog. Although most dogs welcome new members of the family unconditionally, don't leave this up to chance. With Allie and the birth of both our boys, we found many well-thought-out, clever ideas to aid Allie in accepting these "bundles of joy," Kolby and Weston, into our family and our lives. See some of our suggestions at www.alwaysallie.com. Give us your ideas, too.

Chapter 18

Play Like a Dog

Allie loved to go on walks. She loved to play with her Ace-wrapped toy. She liked playing fetch. She enjoyed life. Here's a suggestion for you: Find things you enjoy doing. Recognize those activities that make you happy. Take notes from your pet. Pets understand how to truly enjoy life. The old saying "all work and no play makes Jack a dull boy" is true. Life is filled with stressors. Plenty of them! We spend hours working, trying to get ahead, or to acquire those creature comforts that will enable us to live the "American Dream." There's merit in this. But if that's all you do, then you are cheating yourself of truly enjoying the time you have on this earth. The saying "life is too short" is also true. So, be sure that you enjoy each day. No matter how young or how old you are, make time each and every day to play as Allie did!

Chapter 19
On Alerts and Anxiety

We have all heard of situations where dogs have alerted their owners of impending danger. This is a wonderfully unique, God-given trait that I love about dogs. Tell us your story of how your pooch saved you and your loved ones from a dangerous situation.

You have probably also encountered situations where a dog was afraid of storms, lightning or loud noises, such as firecrackers. There are ways to make these events less intimidating for your sensitive pooch. Go to www.alwaysallie.com and learn some of these techniques and see some of our suggestions for making your dog less anxious. Also, sign up for our online contests and occasional promotional giveaways at www.alwaysallie.com.

Chapter 20
Killer Chocolate?

The veterinary community takes a strong stance that chocolate is harmful to dogs. In our own experience, this rule had not proven absolute. All of our pets have devoured their share of chocolate, and none seemed adversely affected. I'm not advocating that chocolate become a part of the canine recommended daily allowance, but I disagree with the unwavering principle that dogs cannot have chocolate. Allie suffered from Crohn's disease, so her chocolate antics generally caused her intestines more discomfort than the momentary pleasure she gained from it. Unfortunately, she never developed a discerning palate with regard to chocolate. For more information, check out our website, www.alwaysallie.com.

Chapter 21
End-of-Life Planning

How seriously have you thought about euthanasia? This has to be one of the most difficult decisions that an owner makes for his pet. I've been around literally hundreds of euthanasias, and yet it has never gotten easier. Although there are no great suggestions on how to lessen your feelings of loss and sadness, there are some ways to memorialize your pets so that they are never forgotten. Check out our suggestions on how to deal with the emptiness and loneliness upon the death of a pet at www.alwaysallie.com.

Chapter 22
Ages and Stages

You blink, and your puppy has grown old before your very eyes. With Allie, I couldn't believe how the years flew by. Enjoy each and every day with your pet. On our website, we have outlined some of the important milestones in the life of all canines to look for and to enjoy. Do you have some suggestions regarding enjoying your pet each and every day? Tell us your ideas and share with us your personal experiences at www.alwaysallie.com. Also, watch our website for occasional online contests. Sign up for our promotional giveaways at www.alwaysallie.com.

Chapter 23
Got an Alpha Dog?

Be careful of the "alpha" dog. The presence of two "alpha" dogs without close supervision almost certainly leads to trouble. How do you tell which dog is the "alpha"? Is your dog an "alpha" dog? Can dogs change roles based on the situation, or is it an absolute certainty, once an "alpha" always an "alpha"? Find the answers to these questions and more at www.alwaysallie.com.

Chapter 24
Famously Privileged Pups

Just as an adopted child does not choose his parents, the same is true for puppies. In the case of Barney and Spot, with a simple twist of fate, they found themselves in the lap of luxury. It can be entertaining and informative to take a closer look at those few dogs of privilege. At www.alwaysallie.com, we have described several lifestyles of the rich and famous canines who have landed a posh and luxurious position in life. Have you had an opportunity to meet a dog of privilege? Tell us your story and participate in our online contests at www.alwaysallie.com.

Chapter 25
Pampering Is Okay

It's okay to pamper your pooch. Spoil him rotten, especially during his "golden years." Who among us doesn't enjoy being doted on? Allie often encouraged us to coddle her in her own special way, and we generally obliged. Do you pamper your furry friend? In what way? Tell us your story at www.alwaysallie.com.

Chapter 26
Live in the Moment

When I look back over the last five years of Allie's life, I realize that I cheated myself in many respects. I began to observe her physical changes from month to month and realized that she was growing old before my eyes. I was so uncertain about how to deal with these feelings of sadness that I forgot to enjoy her each day. Instead, I was consumed by the thought that she could die any day. Somewhere around the sixteenth year of her life, I realized I was doing this, and also realized I was cheating myself out of valuable time spent with Allie. I made a personal decision and a conscious effort to force these thoughts of dread from my mind.

Don't get caught in this trap in your own life. This can happen with any relationship, whether people or pets. Make the decision that you will not focus on the "what if's" but instead focus on the "I will's!" This decision will serve you well in learning how to enjoy to the fullest extent all of the important people and pets in your life.

Chapter 27

Saying Goodbye

Grieve the loss of your beloved pet. Participate in the final and most important act of kindness, the process of letting your pet go and putting him down. Treat your canine companion just as you want to be treated upon your "deathbed." The Golden Rule truly applies during the golden years. Participating in this final event will likely be one of the most difficult things you will do in this life. But your pet deserves to have his most cherished friend by his side. Even with the unbearable pain, you will be glad you were a part of this final act.

At www.alwaysallie.com, you can read our recommendations regarding end-of-life decisions, pet burial and cremation decisions, final resting-place options (like pet cemeteries and crematoriums) and suggestions for how to deal with grief and loss.

Epilogue
Your Next Dog

After just the right length of time has passed, you will likely wish to get another dog. This is an individualized decision. Give yourself the time that you need to mourn the loss of your loved one. You may want to make this a group decision; remember the entire family is affected by the loss of Fido. Also, consider that each person who decides not to get another dog prevents one more dog from being adopted or experiencing the love and feelings of being a member of a family. You may want to consider getting your next pet from a shelter. There are thousands of dogs who have been abandoned, abused, neglected or lost, or who have outlived their owner and are in desperate need of a home. These shelter or rescue dogs generally make wonderful pets. They seem to understand, inherently, that you have done just that—rescued them from a life of neglect and abuse, and for this they seem to be eternally grateful. At www.alwaysallie.com, we have listed some resources that will help you locate a quality shelter in your area. If you do decide to adopt a rescue dog, know that Allie would be pleased with your selfless decision!

About the Author

I am the youngest of four children, born and raised in the small town of Colby in Western Kansas. My father, now a retired veterinarian, practiced both large and small animal medicine in rural Kansas. Much of my time growing up was spent observing and participating in my father's practice. During these formative years, I gained a keen awareness of the importance that pets can have on our lives. In my opinion, the canine breed is the most interesting and cherished species of pets.

After finishing my undergraduate degree at Bethany College, I returned for a year to my high school alma mater in Colby, where I served as an assistant wrestling and track and field coach. During that year in my hometown, I realized that I had a burning desire to become a doctor. I found myself spending much of my spare time thinking about the various medical specialties. Although altruistic, I recognized a heartfelt desire to help people. My inner self yearned to become part of something bigger than me. I spent some of my spare time shadowing several different physicians in my home town and the surrounding communities. This was time well spent. I recognized that my personal makeup suited a career in medicine.

I was accepted into medical school, and in the fall of 1986 began my medical training at Kansas City University of Medicine and Biosciences. After four years of medical school and an internship, I entered a three-year residency in family medicine.

My desire to live and practice in a small town led me to Weston, Missouri. Here I grew a solo, all-inclusive medical practice, occasionally referred to as a practice from "womb to tomb." During these years I developed an extensive breadth of medical knowledge and experience that enhanced my ability as an interventional radiologist.

After several years practicing rural medicine, I returned to a second four-year residency in diagnostic radiology at Oklahoma State University in Tulsa, Oklahoma. Then I completed a one-year fellowship in interventional radiology at the Washington Hospital Center in Washington, D.C.

As a physician who has triple board certification in interventional radiology, diagnostic radiology and family medicine, I currently practice in Topeka, Kansas, and in the surrounding rural communities. Besides practicing medicine, I am the host of a weekly local medical talk radio show, Doctor's Orders, a one-hour show about interesting topics in medicine.

If the concept that the left brain engages in analytical, concrete thinking is true, my creative and abstract right brain has successfully waged war on my left cerebral hemisphere. My love of music and fine arts has encouraged the development of the right side of my mind. Writing has been an important part of developing my creativity for years.

My family includes my wife, Tracy Gavin Van Camp, and my two sons, Kolby and Weston. After our four-legged daughter, Allie, died in March of 2009, we welcomed Addie, a second Bichon Frise, into the fold in October 2009.

Addie came from Springfield, Missouri, from Yoshi's Bichons. She was a descendent of J.R. the Best in Show National Champion at the 2001 Westminster National Dog Show.

Although pets can have many traits that are similar, they have their unique characteristics that make them special in their own way. I often joke with "Addie" that she has some mighty big paws to fill. But in reality, she can never replace Allie. And I would never expect, nor want, her to try. She will and should be Always Addie.